D1524331

The Fiction of the Poet

The Fiction of the Poet

*FROM MALLARMÉ TO THE
POST-SYMBOLIST MODE*

✜

ANNA BALAKIAN

PRINCETON UNIVERSITY PRESS

PRINCETON, NEW JERSEY

Library of Congress Cataloging-in-Publication Data
Balakian, Anna Elizabeth, 1915–
The fiction of the poet : from Mallarmé to the post-symbolist mode
/ Anna Balakian.
p.   cm.
Includes index.
1. Poetry, Modern—20th century—History and criticism.
2. Mallarmé, Stéphane, 1842–1898—Influence.   3. Symbolism (Literary
movement)   4. Symbolism in literature.
PN1271.B36   1992
ISBN 0-691-06946-8
809.1'915—dc20   91-33525   CIP

This book has been composed in Linotron Galliard

Princeton University Press books are
printed on acid-free paper, and meet the guidelines
for permanence and durability of the Committee
on Production Guidelines for Book Longevity
of the Council on Library Resources

Printed in the United States of America

10   9   8   7   6   5   4   3   2   1

TO THE MEMORY OF MY SISTER

NONA BALAKIAN

✢

To end up in a beautiful book,
that is what the world was made for
—*Stéphane Mallarmé*

✤ Contents ✤

✤ *Acknowledgments* ✤

I AM GRATEFUL for permission from Random House and Faber and Faber to reproduce the works of Wallace Stevens that appear here, and to Professor Donald Friedman for his translations of Stéphane Mallarmé's "Hérodiade" and "L'Après-midi d'un faune"; to Professor Claudio Guillén for his translation of Jorge Guillén's "Presagio"; and to Hugh Creekmore and Richard Wilbur for their translations of selected poems from Guillén's *Cántico*.

The Fiction of the Poet

Introduction

THE SYMBOLIST MOVEMENT that some critics declared to have died at the end of the nineteenth century has survived in many forms. It was a determining factor in the era when it filled an aesthetic and spiritual need. Subsequently it turned art into a constant among variables vis-à-vis the increasing relativity of our perceptions of reality. After the sorting out that time and distance bring about, what indeed remains of the dogma and the epistle of the Symbolist chapel?[1] What really caused the proselytism of the moment and the extended catalytic effect? The search for the answer to these questions motivates my reading of these postsymbolist poets.

Symbolism triggered, first of all, a poetics of language to replace the language of poetry. Through the maze of debates and theories about versification, synaesthesia, correspondences, and the spirit of decadence, there emerged a central problem: what, in the twentieth century, constitutes poetry, in view of the fact that the boundaries of versification and the propriety of subject matter to poetic treatment have been totally eliminated? None of the major features proposed and embodied by the Symbolist group at the end of the nineteenth century have carried over as matters of primary consequence into the twentieth century.

What makes Symbolism and its avatars of interest in current poetics are, then, the elements related to semiotics and herme-

---

[1] As in my previous books and essays on Symbolism, an uppercase *S* will signify the literary movement that took place in Paris between 1885 and 1900. The lowercase *s* will be used in reference to neosymbolism and the symbolist style outside of the chronological boundaries of the movement. Note also that Romanticism and Romantic, when referring to the literary movement, will be in uppercase.

neutics inherent at the source and appropriated by the major poets who distinguished themselves from the vast group of adherents. Among the survivors who have gained prominence with time are Paul Valéry, Rainer Maria Rilke, W. B. Yeats, Wallace Stevens, and Jorge Guillén. They will be viewed here in the perspective of their direct connection with Mallarmé. I am cognizant of the fact that hermeneutic and semiotic criticism has taken renewed interest in the symbolist mode but not in its historical context. Philosophically oriented and linguistically trained critics have approached literary symbolism with a pejorative attitude, and they have reached Mallarmé via a more express route to modern concepts of poetics. Their responses to Mallarmé, perceptive as they are, overlook the factors of continuity and the episteme that connected those who were in the process of rethinking the concept of poetry. Their perceptions of Mallarmé as well as of Valéry support many of the aesthetic issues explored here, but the broader views comprise the connective factors responsible for the greater stature of those

[2] See, for instance, Philippe Sollers's article "Literature and Totality," where he detaches Mallarmé from the "obsolete decadentism of the symbolists," whom he characterizes as a category of minor French poets (in *Writing and the Experience of Limits*, ed. David Hayman [New York, 1983]). In the same anthology of criticism, Paul de Man admits in "Lyrics and Modernity" that "the question of modernity in the lyric is considered as the best means or access to a discussion of literary modernity in general . . . Some of the most suggestive theoretical writing on modernity is to be found in essays dealing with poetry" (64). In this reader's view what is unfortunate is the fact that he accepts the notions of previous eras of criticism that symbolism is the continuation and increasingly morbid version of Romanticism. It is also to be noted that H. R. Jauss acknowledges in *Aesthetic Experience and Literary Hermeneutics* the "semantic plurality" of Mallarmé, as does Jacques Derrida in *Dissemination*, where he uses that expression as a substitute for polysemy. E. S. Burt and Barbara Johnson have also recognized the layering character of meaning in Mallarmé as a positive factor of his *écriture*. But the connection of these traits to the writings of a historically later cluster of major poets has been almost diffidently rejected by hermeneutic critics in general, and by critics, hermeneutic or not, specializing in the individual poets here studied.

whose work contained a slice of the symbolist experience they shared at a certain moment in time.[2]

What strikes me in the progression of the symbolist mode is the passage from allegory (unilateral correspondences) to symbol, from metaphoric closing to the open-ended metonymy, and finally to the evocative power discovered in the single word serving as a prism for associations and significances. We can see in the *écriture* of these major poets a mastery of language that surpasses the skills of rhetoric but becomes instead a low-keyed deployment of the resources of the imagination in direct contrast to the divestment of these same powers from narrative prose.

When so-called postmodern novelists declare the demise of analogy in a universe that offers no correspondences to human goals and desires, the art of representation can no longer be expected to open vistas for the correction of an unsatisfactory reality. Instead, it keeps narrowing the distance between what any person can ascertain and what the "fiction" writer is supposed to illuminate. Zola, as a supposed "naturalist," brought powerful light to the darkest pits he unearthed. But since his time, fiction has passed out of the novel, which is becoming more and more the graphic processing of an assortment of data, resembling a police file, a psychiatric case study, or a slightly altered autobiography. A handful of novelists who still maintain both in the U.S. and abroad the art of finding the luminous in the opacity of the human clay are grossly underread and undervalued in the critical arena.

At a certain moment in time, fiction passed from the practitioners of the narrative genre to poetry as the poet tried to provide, as in the examples given here, what I like to consider a semantic transcendentalism to compensate for the waning of metaphysical yearnings. If we cannot overcome physical barriers to our spiritual needs, and if religions as the traditional escape mechanism are found ineffective, then language becomes the recourse, the mainstay of those adept in its uses, serving the imagination with its capacity to provide runways and exits to its manipulators.

Beneath the fundamental precept of Mallarmé lay an episteme, a collective perception of a philosophical climate affecting a certain time in aesthetic development. Why his famous dictum that the poet must no longer narrate? Narration implies a certain continuity, a sequence, which structures the reality by which Man[3] lives. The opposite of measured time is discontinuous time, dead time, or archeological time—as in the case of Mallarmé's *Hérodiade*—or suspended time—as conveyed by Samuel Beckett, who comes very close to being neither a novelist nor a dramatist but simply a poet.

Thus it comes to pass that fiction, which is normally associated with narrative, takes on an opposite sense in postsymbolist poetics: fiction becomes the totality of the conditions that a poet can control in a universe where nothing can be foreseen or determined in the natural context, and where, according to Guillén, the supreme enemy is "accident."

Rejecting both the natural and supernatural correspondences, the generations of neosymbolists go beyond what Rilke called "the interpreted world," usurping the place of heaven as the site of survival in an augmented parameter for the arts. To do this, they perform a mutation of the known tropes. They do not seek to offer representation, but look for fresh presentations in what Guillén called "the absolute moment" in time that can never again be duplicated. A substitution technique replaces the suggestive one. The word "poet" disappears from the lexicon and is replaced by referents internationally recognizable in the readings of the poets in this study. A destructive approach to connotations occurs, and also a return to denotations or an advance toward new connotations that are understood beyond the linguistic barriers separating these poets. A system gradually emerges of which we are not immediately aware. It

---

[3] It is to be noted that "Man" is used throughout this work as the equivalent of "the human species," inclusive of all genders and sexual persuasions.

seems as if the poet, sickle in hand, were demolishing the signi-
fieds not to eliminate the established sociopolitical codes, but
rather to destroy the existential meanings, to revise the role of
Man, the artist, and beyond that the function of just plain Man
as the receiver of the artist's communication. Probably the most
important discovery of symbolists throughout the world is that
true and deep communication does not occur through the simple process of uniting the thought of the writer with that of the
reader. Instead, there occurs an exploration of the possibilities
of prismatic dissipations in the path of communication in the
form of objects, sites, people. Finally, naked words used in isolation generate a scale of ambiguities that increase the range
and depth of communication. One might even suggest that poetic communication as developed in the symbolist mode contains a subversive intent. Indeed, it is often implicitly persuad-
ing the reader of a truth diametrically opposed to the obvious
meaning of the words employed.

Through these tactics, poets provide us with much enlight-
enment on the very nature of communication as it ceases to be
the receiving of information or the sharing of a specific emotion. Instead, language in the new poetic sense becomes a place
of encounter for analogies that are to the enrichment of personality what an interlining is to a simple cloth garment. Communication between the poet and the reader is composed of those
images that are proposed by the poet and those generated by
the reader to whom the author has given the responsibility of
creating implicit rather than explicit interpretations.

The position assumed, historically, by the neosymbolists all
over the world was an intermediary step between a form of art
in which cryptograms were presumed to be decipherable and
that ultimate and transparent void that is being declared by certain writers of our own end-of-century, who no longer tolerate
any kind of analogical pact, whether it be between God and
Man or between the poet and his readers.

Situated between two extremes, the writers selected here as
representative of postsymbolists did not choose to interpret

that enigma; they created it in freeing the signifier from its commitment to any particular signified, by a return to the etymological source, or by the destruction of clichés and the substitution of one referent for the other. There are no limits to the horizons of expectation for works that surpass the possibilities of preordained representation.

We see emerging here a selective system of communication that relates directly to the philosophical preoccupations of the critical mind. Without expounding any particular philosophy, and indeed without intent at clarification, it identifies the realms of human resistance to spiritual annihilation. The poets signaled here are among the most prominent of a vast constellation of which many are lost to critical recognition because they belong to unfamiliar literatures. Engrossed as these poets all were with the powers of language, they did not use it as a pretext for word games, but rather to posit the major problems of existence and its survival.

The factors relating to affiliation are much more complex than the pursuit of direct and avowed influences. There are exterior elements that bind writers and artists together, such as prevalent mentalities (the trembling of the veil in this instance, the last whimpers over the loss of the anthropocentric universe, the impact of sociopolitical events).

There are also strata formations from parallel intellectual developments among individual writers of separate national cultures. Certainly this is true of poets who all read Baudelaire without necessarily reading one another's writings or read Mallarmé, Freud, or Marx; and to go beyond common readings, how many are the books we talk about and think we know about without ever having read them! What we call an intellectual climate is this collective assimilation of ideas that predominate in a given moment in time.

One fact clearly emerges from all the comparative readings I have done, which, I believe, justifies the network I have established here: Symbolism slipped out of France both as a direct imitation and as a more creative transformation, and the cluster of poets who loom as major voices a century later are those who bypassed the technical innovations and discarded the congealed meanings of the collective paradigms to extract their gold from the source—that is, who made their personal applications of the basic theories and works of Mallarmé. In most instances the symbolist *écriture* became one of many arteries of nourishment for a poetry that created a mosaic of dense and complex works. Each unique in his way, these solitaries, here viewed in serial readings, possesses a common interface—the symbolist mode.

A Serial Approach

Tнᴇ ᴍᴀᴊᴏʀ critical phenomenon in late twentieth-century criticism has been the practice of far-flung intertextuality that juxtaposes distant literary realities and at the same time demonstrates a traumatic fear of seeking out influences. In that light the current study of poetic proximities will appear conventional. In my previous critical scholarly writings, my primary objective has been the straightforward and pragmatic task of unfolding information about unfamiliar or neglected texts, focusing on survivals of value out of the indiscriminate miscellany of literary movements; I have used geographical and temporal distance to gauge qualities that have prevailed beyond the historical moment of first reader perception. I have aimed for a delicate balance in the case of both Symbolism and surrealism between poetic intentions and critical responses. Above all, my own methodological approach has been historical and texts have been read in context.

Sometimes my objectivity has been questioned, though I have never used the personal "I" or qualified any mode or person with superlatives. But I suppose that *choice* is in itself a symptom of predilection. Seldom do critics choose to write about an author they detest, or even for whom they have no empathy. I must admit that my choices have been marginal to the popular scholarly preferences. I have highlighted what I considered the neglected authors—that is, those who were neglected at the time that I ventured to write about them. Even the Symbolists, who had enjoyed much popularity in the 1920s, had slipped into the purgatory of temporary oblivion when I chose to reappraise the movement some years ago.[1] On

---

[1] See Anna Balakian, *The Symbolist Movement: A Critical Appraisal* (New York, 1967; revised ed., New York, 1977); also *The Symbolist Movement in*

11

the whole, time has been supportive of my choices. I never wrote about Flaubert, Joyce, or even Virginia Woolf, and attempted only one essay on Proust[2] because I felt that scholarship was overloading those writers, and it was especially heavy on the novel in general. I felt that I could be more useful if I focused my responses on poetic writings. Because the subjects of my scholarship were among the less familiar literary outputs of the nineteenth and twentieth centuries, I adopted the informative style and developed techniques of synthesis to cover vast bodies of writing within few pages as an alternate current to the specific textual probes in which I engaged. I saw no purpose in presenting analyses of restricted texts that often were not available to my readers, or, in the case of foreign literatures, not available in translation. As justification for my work, I felt that sometimes it is more useful to the noninformed reader to gain a general sense of the work and its spirit through the eyes of a critic who has absorbed the total body of the writing than through a speedy or inaccurate translation. If with this second-hand knowledge interested readers will later approach the translation, they will be in a better position to deal with it, as it were, with a grain of salt. I have tried to be that grain of salt for those whose first experiences with Symbolism and surrealism have been through my writings. We talk of the Work of a creative writer as a totality. I think that the questions I have probed and tried to answer in the course of my long career as a scholarly essayist have, in establishing a continuity between these two major literary movements that have spanned a century, given my own work a certain unity.

Now, in the postmeridian stage of my critical studies, I will indulge in the critical "I" and deal with some of the same materials I have previously approached historically, but this time

---

the *Literature of European Languages*, ed. Anna Balakian (Budapest, 1982), for historical delimitations and distinctions in manner of passage to various other nations and cultures.

[2] Anna Balakian, "Proust Fifty Years Later," in *Comparative Literature Studies* 10 (June 1973): 93–111.

from a serial point of view, from which continuity is no longer considered merely a product of chronology but as consortial elaborations and transformations, demonstrating the fact—which I proposed many years ago—that the connotation of the word "influence" has gone awry,[3] confused with the word "imitation." Many studies on the impact of Symbolism and of Mallarmé on the major poets of various nations have either treated the subject in a defensive manner, categorically proclaiming the absence of such influence, or assumed a subservient attitude vis-à-vis the original in an effort to prove that the unknown poet strictly belonged in the league. True influence is transformation, in my view. It is not subjected to some kind of psychological repression, but is contingent on the inevitable exhaustion of the original model, or on the evolution of forms, both organic and semantic. These changes or avatisms of models are not necessarily assumed to be improvements over the originals even as we know now, in view of recent scientific studies, that in the case of biological evolution the changes that occur are not presumed to follow a code of progress.

But the serial variations and elaborations in the span between Symbolism and surrealism touch on the very nature of poiesis. I am borrowing the word "serial" from the terminology of contemporary music, in which it applies to techniques of composition. I am using the term in the context of literary affiliations that, like tone rows in serial music, return to their original base periodically to advance from it to transformations preserving a certain acoustic unity. Although the original term applies to the coordination of the parts of a single composition, by analogy one can propose a methodology that explores the possibility of coordinating a cluster of poets into an interreferential system that preempts their individual linguistic expression. Thus the onus of influence[4] can be lifted from the gravitations that these poets experienced toward Mallarmé's quiet

[3] Anna Balakian, "Influence and Literary Fortune," in *Yearbook of Comparative Literature*, no. 11 (Bloomington, Ind., 1962).

[4] Our current generation of Comparatists is in a quandary about organization and methodology. Its members are told to shy away from influence stud-

revolution that attempted to break away from traditional modes of poetic communication. As we proceed from one poet to the next in this study, we perceive the serial progress that amid wide differences creates a certain cohesion among them.

It is disturbing to me that an expression pertaining to semiotics—"a surplus of meaning"—is being used in literary criticism, concerning the nature of metaphor and symbol, to suggest that in this form of communication there is an excess of meaning to be dealt with. If the meaning of meaning is closely grasped in relation to poetry, it is readily evident that the notion of "surplus" is intolerable and inconceivable. For, precisely, in poetic communication the well of meaning is inexhaustible because meaning is not linear, but rather a circular vortex in perpetual motion. A poem that does not attain such a pool of meaning is a failed poem. This perception of poetics is, in the long run, the most important contribution that the original Symbolist group under the impetus of Mallarmé made to the redefinition of poetry, and the impact of this concept upon several generations of poets over and above national frontiers has been so strong that the symbolist notion of poetry has become the sine qua non of effective, viable poetry thereafter. "The margin of surplus," as Derrida calls what he perceives as a series of valences to the main track of meaning, assumes in reality a basic minimum requirement for poetic writing, and the fundamental contribution of Mallarmé and his followers to poetics was to assert and demonstrate that the communication of a message in direct discourse no longer constituted poetry.

---

ies and thematic approaches and move toward a freer intertextuality. But most intertexual studies have become too free and too arbitrary. Here I have tried to offer a model of intertexuality in which filiation blends with affiliation and a set of comparisons cannot be justified merely on the basis of the personal predilections of the critic or even on the basis of shared ideas. Poets talk to each other and to us in terms of imagery and they pursue, through a convention of metaphors, their reflections on life. They thus approach, like painters and composers of music recurrences of imagery that transcends their native language communications.

The so-called surplus was no longer to be considered an excess but rather the essential ingredient for poetic viability. The mechanism at work, which gave the innocent reader a sense of "surplus," is at the heart of the Symbolist technique and continues in great measure to be at the core of surrealist poetry as well, although in terms of philosophical perspectives and assumptions of life-style the two movements have been antithetical.

The Symbolists cultivated this impression of "surplus" of meaning by mastering the art of ambiguity, by sucking away at the roots of etymological meaning, by deconstructing congealed connotations. In a later generation, André Breton continued the task with his notion of "les mots sans rides" [words without wrinkles],[5] which was the positive side of the search for new meanings in a language of excessive poetic conventions. In other words, if connotations overladen or eroded with frequent use have lost the elasticity to suggest the possibility of "surplus" meaning, if the bag of meaning has truly been emptied, then the words themselves may have lost their poetic usefulness and should be laid to rest in favor of others heretofore not subjected to poetic service and therefore capable of encompassing a proliferation of meanings. Since the moment of Rimbaud's sigh to find a new language (in his letter to his teacher, Demeny), it is a prescription for all seekers of the meaning of poetry to look for that comprehension within language itself, the common, depleted treasure, rather than to believe that changes in philosophical and psychological attitudes alone can replenish the poetic vision.

The poet's attitude toward poiesis has in fact run counter to the direction that poetry criticism takes when it ventures into psychological explanations, and associates or even confuses literary symbol with the Freudian or other psychosemantic symbolism. The psychological symbol has been used to crystallize the ineffable, involuntary motivations and desires inherent in

---

[5] André Breton, "Les Mots sans rides," in *Les Pas Perdus* (Paris, 1924).

human behavior. Poetry is a most lucid activity, a spreading of a fan of meanings, the vivid perception of the vituperations of the word strategically placed, or the image fortuitously achieved. The surrealist Breton aptly called this situation "magnetic fields," which attract reception and provide vistas leading to the extension of the capacities and variations of language not only for the reader but also for the creator of the work, who beholds with wonder what has been created. Thus receiving one's own image leads to an extension, for the image is no longer considered merely a reflection, of either the conscious state or the subconscious. Valéry sought to define this process of exceeding the mirror of self in his Narcissus poems, as we shall observe later on.

Whereas Freudian methodology becomes increasingly used in the study of literature, it will be excluded from these considerations except as a historical phenomenon concurrent with poetic developments. This particular study of perceptions is based on the hypothesis that poetry is primordially a reversal of the pedestrian use of *language* in favor of the literary function to transform the real world into a fiction. It is curious that the word *fiction* has for so long become associated with prose rather than with poetry. Even in the most fantastic and imaginative writings in the novel form, the connection of the romanesque with reality is more evident (although it is often considered tangential) than in the case of poetry in its most realistic vein.

The true fiction is that of the poet, as Mallarmé so intelligently perceived. As no one before him, he opened up the processes of creating that fiction, which, with the words of the world of realities and with the mechanics of their communication, achieves that level of artifice implied by his famous statement about the flower "absent from all bouquets" as the epitome of pure poetic creation. Naming, said Mallarmé in *Variations sur un sujet*, does not evoke a return of any particular contour of which we have empirical knowledge and that is specifically recognizable to us in its natural environment; instead, the act of naming, which is synonymous with creating, is the composite or the *virtual* image made possible by an art *dedicated to fictionalization*: "le dire retrouve chez le Poète, par nécessité constitutive d'un art consacré aux fictions sa virtualité" [speaking recovers in the poet, by the constituent necessity of an art devoted to fictions, its virtuality], and the object concrete but not specific is "bathed in a new atmosphere." It should be noted that Mallarmé does not use the word "nouvelle," which would have suggested mere displacement from one context to another, but "neuve," meaning brand-new or fresh—that is, fictitious, a confection. Many were the examples of his dictum to be discovered in the poetry not of the Symbolist *cénacle* but of a later generation—of which several are singled out in this work, whose primary purpose is to show that influence or filiation can occur on different levels in successive generations who drink at the same source. Sometimes those somewhat distanced from the catalyst either temporally or geographically can be affected on a deeper level than those too close.

When readers accept the notion of the absent flower, the effect is not to spur them to go out in the fields to look for the unnamed flower; instead they become surrounded by the image of the absent one, which in its anonymity becomes a turbulent presence. The perception of the imperceptible occurs not through a distorting lens but by a rational adaptation to an unexpected linguistic association—in this case, the adjective's annulling the communication of the noun. In another such instance, the fictitious is achieved by the verb denying the reality expressed by the noun—"vols qui n'ont pas fui," in Mallarmé's sonnet "Le vierge, le vivace et le bel aujourd'hui"—which is a simple grammatical structure communicating a negation of experience. What is the good of discovering the psychological reasons for the very obvious frustration that might have given rise to Mallarmé's enunciation? Psychology may explain the state of mind that provokes such human communication, but it cannot explain the structures of the poetic discourse put to use to convey it. The poetic fact is that the metonymy of "flights that have not flown" conjures an image of flight that negates its own function through a linguistic device that by its precision opens the doors wide to the reader's reception of the experience of the poet. To share is not the primary aim of this poetic communication, but to stimulate imaginative speculation on the part of the reader. The ambiguity of the literary denotation unleashes the memory of an infinite number of precisions on the part of the reader. The fiction of the poet is the suggestion of an unusual runway for impossible flights described as non-flights, which, because of the precise generalization, can be implemented by an unlimited number of personalized images created by the reader. This simple illustration shows that meaning is not necessarily an equation between emission and reception, but in its richer sense becomes a radiation from the poet to an infinite number of unpredictable antennas; for the precise invariable statement annuls any possibility for specificity of relation between sender and receiver.

Since from Symbolism on all authentic poetry is essentially polysemous, all exegeses are intellectual exercises that serve several purposes, all lying outside of the appreciation of poetry itself. They may clarify the critic's own psyche, becoming a substitute for personal therapy; they may serve as gymnastics for building up mental muscle; they may elucidate biographical facts about the poet; they may clarify for other readers ambiguities of references to myths or to geographical allusions. They are rarely useful as a demonstration of the process of creation, which in my opinion is the highest priority of aesthetic criticism and which, in its pragmatic justification, should lead to the awakening of imaginative qualities in the reader. It is true, however, that the intricacies of some exegeses do give an insight into the riches of the poem itself in its finite dimensions—if not into its generating force and its capacity to trigger the imagination of the reader. Short of this ultimate end relating to the aesthetic experience, there are scholarly activities that can prepare the ground: the exploration of the historical context, classification, clarification of references, discovery of kinships and spiritual climates, and the poet's or poem's epistemological intentions and rhetorical practices. Exegeses can indirectly suggest the multiplicity of meanings but cannot discover *the* meaning—that is, if it is a good poem.

I have practiced many of these activities in dealing with poetry. Now, going over familiar ground, I want to try to isolate the "fiction" of the poetry in observing the central system of poetic motion whereby a particular ontology translates itself into poetry, and is as distinct from theories of writing as it is from philosophical postulations.

If this seriated study were structured in a historical framework I would call it "postsymbolist," since it deals with poets who are the avatars of the Symbolist *cénacle* and who lived in the period following the one identified as "Symbolist." But I am loath to use the prefix "post-" because it suggests the waning or end of something—whereas in this "afterglow" basked such giants as Valéry, Rilke, Yeats, Stevens, and Guillén, who constituted a flowering that, like September roses, had greater splendor and fuller body than before, since these poets used in original ways the tropes and conventions they had inherited from their predecessors. In their transcendence, however, of the symbolist tradition they developed successive verbal maneuvers and strategies that consolidated the fiction of the poet.

The major poets of the twentieth century moved in a direction diametrically opposed to that of writers of prose narrative. The modern novel does not exploit irreality even in its most preposterous manifestations of so-called fantasy. It deepens reality by appropriating the subconscious perceptions and amalgamating them with the conscious. We have been told that the unconscious is a dragnet of reality. Involuntary memory, once awakened, is not too remote from the voluntary, although it is less organized and more luminous. The stream of unconscious discourse changes the conventional order of communication—it sometimes fragments syntax, it plunges often into the scatological—but it is identifiable as reality in its data, in its semantics, and is open to psychological analysis. The disorders of time sequence demand some adaptation in the reading process, but once the adjustment is made the reader still has the sensation of the flow of time, whether reversed or simultaneous. Dream sequences, as psychologists have informed us, are based in reality or in waking experience and can readily be translated back into normal cognizance. When all else fails in our effort to grasp meaning, as in the case of the "nouveau roman," our confounded attitude toward our failure suggests that we suppose the author to have intended direct communication with us and that on our part there arises a need and expectation to seize that direct meaning. We tend to turn the relationship into a guessing game or an effort at mind reading. When this relationship is categorically denied by the author and no longer expected by the reader, it is to be admitted that the novelist is moving into the realm of poetry, as indeed Alain Robbe-Grillet and Claude Simon have done in the best of their work. I can go so far as to say that this strategic transgression has been producing better poetry of late than a host of so-called poets who are indulging in facile word associations gleaned from romanesque mimesis. In an exchange of functions, they have become prose writers in free linear form and have deserted the fiction of poetic discourse discovered by the poets of the early twentieth century.

My critical attitude toward the appropriation of the so-called subconscious by modern poets will surprise those who know of my fascination with surrealism, which has been defined by its creators and its explicators as the expression of reality in its deeper and highly overcharged sense. But in terms of the creation of poetry, I would venture to state that the truest poets in the surrealist coterie surpass in their poetic practices the surrealist ontology of which they may be exemplary representatives in their daily existence. In the case of certain poets nurtured by Symbolism, the opposite occurred; Wallace Stevens and Jorge Guillén ended up by rejecting the symbolist philosophical attitudes—or, as in the case of Valéry, they moved away from it while they developed the techniques that crystallized the fiction of the poet.

In trying to maintain a comparatist optic, I shall focus on aspects of the poetic character of these poets that minimize their particular national heritages. Mallarmé, it is true, rises out of the French exploration of rhetoric, of the refinement of the academic baggage of literary references, and of the collective mythopoiesis of French writing. Valéry continues in the same path. It is equally true that Rilke belongs to the Germans, and that the whole German Romantic tradition is inculcated in him. The German philosophies have left an undeniable impact on Rilke, and he has been studied in that context so often that it may be foolhardy to view him in any other light. Yeats and Wallace Stevens have been so definitively related to the Anglo-American poetic tradition that it will almost seem as if I am dealing with totally different poets. I know of Yeats's debt to William Blake, and that the *Vision* would not have been possible without *Eskial*. But I am not interested at the moment in the *Vision* and in the particular associated forms of the Kaballa and Gnosticism with which Yeats has become linked by readers who have read critical commentary about him. Simply speaking, I am not interested in Yeats's *thinking*. When I want communication about philosophical thought I like to go to those who practice thinking professionally—that is, the philosophers. I am not interested in Nietzsche's philosophy through Yeats's misinterpretations. But reaching down into the prime matter that was elaborated in Nietzsche's thought, I want to see how it became manifest in poetic composition in Yeats's "The Second Coming" or elsewhere. And knowing that Yeats was recuperating from a severe illness when he wrote "The Second Coming" may explain some of his attitudes inherent in the poem, which is legitimate information about Yeats that helps create a certain empathy in me for the human being vibrant in the poet. But that knowledge does not in itself transform the depressed human being into a tragic poet.

Biography is a fascinating approach to the understanding of a poet, but it does not explain his poetry. So, in this instance, Yeats will be for us a gear in a process, in the poetic process, and in that sense he will be a universal phenomenon, detached and freed from national attributes and encumbrances—fascinating and enriching though the national factors may be in the total consideration of the author. In parallel fashion, Wallace Stevens's association with Emersonian transcendentalism is a legitimate revelation, but it is a manifestation of a part of him that ties him to the past. And to focus on the poetics involves the isolation of those elements of his poetry pertinent to the *écriture*, in the symbolist context. In this respect the late Michel Benamou made remarkable strides. In his book on Wallace Stevens[6] he focused on Stevens's use of language; he would probably have pursued his study further were it not for his untimely death. As in the case of Edgar Allan Poe, the French perspective is different not because of a disagreement in interpretation of the same writings, but in the evaluation that emerges from the fact that what was interesting to the French in Poe at a certain moment in the development of poetics was quite different from the focus of the Anglo-American critics. There is the same shift of perspective in treating Stevens in a comparative context.

There are poets who are hard to deal with because they do not fit into coteries; they tend to fall between classifications—and, as we know, it is so much easier to explain the unknown in terms of the known that when something does not fit into the pattern of the known data, its author becomes marginal, not as a poet but as a target of criticism. As we read Jorge Guillén's own explanation of what his poetry is about we find in the introduction of *Cántico* both the expected and the unexpected. In terms of the expected, he reiterates what most Spanish writers do—his indebtedness to the Spanish heritage, his sense of generations, or cohabitation in a climate more regional than universal by his own perception—though, interestingly, he wrote the earliest pieces of *Cántico* in Brittany and not in Madrid. He further conveys the expected by giving us the *ideas*

---

[6] See Michel Benamou, *L'Oeuvre-Monde de Wallace Stevens* (Paris, 1975).

contained in his poetry. Yet the unexpected, which interests us at the moment, is also contained there: the notion that poetry is creation and that "the poem should be, word by word, image by image, intensely poetic." Although, unhappily, he associates his own cult of the image with the so-called imagists of New England, I hope to show in his poetry the kind of "image" that is not an actual perception clothed in rhetoric but a semantic device creating a bridge between his inner model and the exterior world.

This group of individual poets lends itself to the probing of the nature of poetry rather than that of verse, and eclectically chosen illustrations reveal the most basic contribution of the Symbolist movement to the art of poetry. The justification of the intertextuality lies not so much in shared philosophical attitudes or in the selection of a special set of images and the pursuit of their survival. It will rather reveal the choice of codes of poetic expression that emerged as the essential catalysts of creativity. If the language of Symbolism appears to reflect a certain ontology, what is truly significant in the literary sense is the fact that the ontology created a new language for poetry and a revised notion of the nature and function of poetic language. If there existed a dichotomy between Symbolism and surrealism in terms of their inherent philosophies of life and objectives of writing, some of that contradiction vanishes into unity when this body of major poets of the first half of the twentieth century is viewed through the *writing* rather than through the *thinking*, in terms of a shared aesthetic experience. Since so much of current poetry is indiscriminately ideological or profusely descriptive communication, it may be appropriate at this time to remind the practicing poet and the reader of the bumper crop of contemporary poetry that there are vast distances between the poetics of fiction and the fiction of poetry.

The Fictions of Mallarmé

> . . . situated at the junctions of all the other
> arts, sprung from them and governing
> them, Fiction or Poetry . . .
> —from *Crayonné au théâtre* (in speaking of Wagner)

MALLARMÉ ESCAPED from History, according to Yeats's observation in "The autumn of the Body," and in the broad sense one might say that he freed himself of ordinary notions of the passage of time. His sparse but dense work is the monument of the drama in which the struggle against the shackles of time resulted in the partial success of the work compensating for the partial failure of the life. He transferred the burden of living upon writing. The writing did the living, better able to sustain the contradictions and inconsistencies of his being than the life pattern to which circumstances over which he had partial but not total control had constricted him: a life that he sums up in his short autobiographical note to Verlaine as "devoid of anecdotes. . . . I probe and find nothing else, the daily troubles, the joys, except for the interior mournings" (664).[1]

Orphaned by the loss of parents, grandparents, and siblings, and orphaned in another sense by the loss of faith in the divine parenthood, he fell into the responsibilities of early marriage and early parenthood, and consequently needed to rely on a profession that might give him outward respectability but meager financial support and virtually no mobility. The contempt

---

[1] It is to be noted that all quotations from Mallarmé, Rimbaud, and Valéry are from the definitive Pléiade edition (Paris, n.d.), and all translations from the French, German, and Spanish are my own except where otherwise indicated.

with which his contemporary, Arthur Rimbaud, viewed seden-tary people in one of his early poems, "Les Assis," was no doubt shared by Mallarmé: "Ces vieillards ont toujours fait tresse avec leurs sieges" ("Les Assis," 37). But unlike his fellow poet, who chose the life of the wanderer and took to the road, Mallarmé shared permanently the lot of the Assis "braided to their seats" as a teacher in the French secondary school system and as a moral man committed to the support of the family he created.

In the same autobiographical note he stresses the fact that he comes from "a line of bourgeois ancestors dating back to the French Revolution" in the form of "an uninterrupted series of civil servants" (661). No winged feet here to take him off to Abyssinia or some unpopulated island waiting to be appropri-ated by him. His famous early poem about the desire for flight, "Brise marine," is a wish to remain ever unfulfilled but also an important factor in the creation of his fictions: nothing, he says, will hold him back—not the light of his writing table, or his young wife nursing their child; he would pull anchor to di-rect his masts toward an exotic place even at the risk of getting lost: "Perdus, sans mâts, sans mâts, ni fertiles îlots . . . / Mais, ô mon coeur, entends le chant des matelots!" But in reality, "fuir! là-bas fuir" is a cry that will have its satisfaction only through the pen in Mallarmé's subsequent works. As I have stated earlier, through the transcendence offered by language, a more sophisticated phase of the realization of desire through language was to be manifested than in the overt terms of "Brise marine" reminiscent of Baudelaire and the Romantics.

The only flights for such as he were to be the flights that have not flown, as those of his pure swan trapped in the ice and immobilized in the dream as more fully expressed in the later sonnet "Le vierge, le vivace et le bel aujourd'hui":

> Ce lac dur oublié que hante sous le givre
> Le transparent glacier des vols qui n'ont pas fui!
>
> . . . .

Fantôme qu'à ce lieu son pur éclat assigne.
Il s'immobilise au songe froid de mépris
Que vêt parmi l'exil inutile le Cygne.

[This hard frozen and forsaken lake which under the cover of its
ice is haunted / by the transparent glacier of flights unflown / . . .
/ A phantom whose pure luster has assigned to this place. / He is
immobilized in a coldly scornful dream / assumed in futile exile
by the Swan.]

What liberty remains to one in his predicament? Only that of
language! But that language becomes for Mallarmé the philosopher's stone, the key to all else that he could be said to have
missed. He compares his stance to the patience of the ancient
alchemist who burned the beams of his house to feed the flame
of the furnace that fashioned the Great Work, that book of
books that was meant to compensate him for everything else
missed.

But before we proceed to unravel the bounties afforded by
language, let us first note that Mallarmé did not even come by
the gift of language easily. The heaviness of much of his prose
suggests the difficulties he had in communicating ideas. The
ponderous sentence structure is not an affectation in Mallarmé
as it often appears to be in late twentieth-century "creative"
criticism; it is symptomatic of blockage, of an autocritical surveillance that impedes the flow of natural speech, a crowding of
ideas that creates a stoppage of circulation, an impasse in the
way of selection of priorities among ideas demanding simultaneous elaboration. Although Mallarmé ironed out much of this
verbal tension in his poetry during the course of the many revi-
sions to which he subjected it in a lifetime of editing, many of
the obscurities that remain in the poetry as well as in the prose
are due to the fact that he makes such a gigantic demand on
language. One has but to read the introduction to his study of
the English language to realize that the history of language is
for Mallarmé an epic venture, each modification a magnificent

heroic act of the human will, a triumph on a bloody battlefield of power play, each transformation a milestone in the construction of the edifice of the humanities. "All acts, complex or quite forgotten obediently resumed for you alone, mindful of your history: a most noble objective and completely philosophical; simple at first then founded on the assumption that in a certain age or in the current era what little we understand depends on our comprehension or on our grasp of some relationships among many things. The gift suffices, but method counts as well—and it emerges from whoever has shaped or will shape his 'humanities'" (900).

For Mallarmé language is a physical body of bone and flesh:

> Related to the entirety of nature and thus closely binding itself
> to the depository organism of life, the Word looms in its vowels
> and diphthongs, like a piece of flesh; and in its consonants, like
> a bone structure disposed to delicate dissection. If life feeds on
> its own past, or on a continual death, Science retrieves this fact
> in language: which, distinguishing man from the rest of things,
> will still imitate him in his fictitious and yet natural essence: de-
> liberate yet fatal, voluntary yet blind. (901)

Each possession of the pleasures can afford is the metaphor of a sexual act of possession, its product a living creation as demonstrated in Mallarmé's poem "Don du poème," in which the labor of a single progenitor in the guise of a literary creator is far more fraught with effort than that of a woman laboring to give birth to a child conceived in double parenthood.

Many of Mallarmé's poems have been subjected to exegeses. Some of his analysts proceed in arbitrary fashion, claiming that there is but one very hidden but penetrable meaning to these abstruse texts. Others, particularly of late, have come around to the belief that such unknown but knowable significances, were they to exist in Mallarmé's poetic writings, would defeat his aim at open-ended ambiguity, and that the "how" in his ambivalence is more important than either the "why" or the "what" that can be gleaned. I believe I was the first in American criticism to pore over *Igitur* in my book *Literary Origins of Surrealism*[2] and I have attempted here and there in my subsequent writings to suggest the meaning of certain details in that "grimoire." But my purpose here is to draw attention not to specific meanings but to the devices that remind readers constantly, in the course of their readings, of the battle Mallarmé waged against the real as he sought to arrive at his fictitious but concrete image of extended existence. "The bourn from which no traveler returns," as Hamlet suggested in his fear of suicide, is the place where Mallarmé proposed to enter and from which to return through the miracle of language.

To illustrate the climate of a living fiction, *Hérodiade* and *The Afternoon of a Faun* are the most appropriate and, interestingly, have been bypassed by many exegetes.[3] "Le vierge, le vivace et le bel aujourd'hui" and the *Coup de dés* support the elements gleaned in the two earlier poems, and in referring to those works I hope to refrain from burdening them with my own subconscious responses and recollections, or my own baggage of literary references.[4]

[2] Anna Balakian, *Literary Origins of Surrealism* (New York, 1947).

[3] Those who have commented on *Hérodiade* have dwelt particularly on the circumstances of its gestation and, selectively, on the design of the language. Especially interesting and prevailing after so many commentaries are Emilie Noulet's observations, in *L'Oeuvre poetique de Stéphane Mallarmé* (Paris, 1940), of the musical structure of the Overture, which, like opera overtures, includes a number of the leitmotifs that reappear in the rest of the composition. Noulet carried the parallel further in observing that the virtual lexicon characteristic of Mallarmé's future work is spelled out here. Such well-known authorities on Mallarmé as Charles Mauron and Jean-Pierre Richard used the text of *Hérodiade* to illustrate themes, imagery, and philosophical attitudes of interpretation of *Hérodiade* by pointing out the absence of certain elements conveniently associated in general with poetic and dramatic analysis. (See *The Death of Stéphane Mallarmé* [New York, 1982]). The most comprehensive attempt at exegesis of this work is that of Robert Greer Cohn, which includes a study of themes, images, and associable references to other interpretations, as well as interior references to other writings of Mallarmé.

[4] I am not referring to *Les Noces d'Hérodiade* as a matter of principle. It was one of the many fragments left by Mallarmé. Since he made an issue of cor-

None of the explanations given so far for Mallarmé's naming his major heroine "Hérodiade," at a time when all his contemporaries were writing and painting around the mytho-religious character of Salome, seem valid to me. Obviously, he was not writing about Salome's mother, who in all historically oriented reference books was called Hérodiade. His own answer to queries was that she was a dream figure independent of history. But in my opinion that was too easy an explanation. I see a reason that was more closely connected with his notion of poetic writing. In renaming Salome Hérodiade, Mallarmé was using one of at least three methods he developed of deconstructing reality and constructing his own fictitious world after accepting a neutral universe. The three evasions we meet all along the labored poetry of Mallarmé are the existential, the referential, and the connotational. Let me elaborate before we enter into specific cases.

The existential is the most obvious. The young man of twenty who said in "Brise marine," " The flesh is sad, alas, and I have read all the books," must have had deep-seated frustrations to spurn so early the pleasures of physical and mental experience. I say "must have" although I know that much psychocriticism has centered around the meager physical experiences of Mallarmé to make the above statement more than a conjecture. But I maintain the "must have" because the facts of his life are of no concern except as reflected in the work, and are the lesser factor between the actual condition and the degree of its penetration into the work. There are poets—to quote Rimbaud, "so many egotists declare themselves poets"—who state

---

recting his work over and over again throughout his life, my respect for his search for perfection makes me loath to evaluate what he refused to acknowledge as a definitive part of his creative output. I find that there is too much time spent by scholars on variants and pre- or posttexts when there remains so much work to be done on the definitive texts. What the French call "avant-texte" has a legitimate value only as a supportive document for verification of chronology, or for psychological factors, none of which are relevant to the aesthetic elements here scrutinized.

such frustrations in squaring the number directly into their work. What Mallarmé's work reveals of the relation between life experience and its reflection in poetry is its *existence*, not the degree of inflation or reduction of the facts. In order to ascertain how deep was the magnification of the frustration, we would have to know something about his capacity for physical experience, which the most astute psychiatrist cannot tell us *after the fact*. The commentator's first and perhaps only function is to try to reveal the dimensions in breadth and depth of the artistic process whose connection with life is only initial and tangential. What we can try to ascertain about the work is the degree of realization of the writer's intention; clearly expressed, that the subjectivity of the writer of the work must be absorbed into the work itself: "L'oeuvre pure implique la disparition elocutoire du poète,qui cède l'initiative aux mots, par le heurt de leur inégalité mobilisés" [The pure work implies the elocutionary disappearance of the poet, who yields the initiative to the words mobilized by the shock of their inequality] ("Crise de vers," 366). Mallarmé is saying that he wants to replace the elocutionary character of verse, which focuses on the subjectivity of the poet, with a method that releases words to their own liberty to align in unequal value according to their natural shocks.

In *Hérodiade* Mallarmé is using his verbal powers to express a state of perilous stagnation of which he had some experience, without a doubt, but which invades and dominates a world of his creation in which his readers can participate to the degree of their own powers of imagination.

The second evasion is the referential. A standard man in many respects, certainly not a bohemian in lifestyle, and trained with the academic tools of his time, Mallarmé cannot conceive of a poetry devoid of cultural references of which a large measure is the common pool of Greek mythology and Biblical allusions. They were a major part of his standard equipment without which he could not consider exercising his art. But there are subtle ways of avoiding references while appearing to use them: using them in unexpected ways, misplacing them, deterring them from expected meanings. The suffix "-iade" has a collective meaning; it designates "the family of." Homer's epic is known as the *Iliad*. In imitation, Voltaire wrote *La Franciade* as an epic of the heritage of France, involving the destiny of more than a single individual. In *Hérodiade* it is apparent to me that Mallarmé is talking of the *family* that produced the emblematic character of Salome, for our vision is first directed to a place and to almost archeological evidences of a family history with an incrustation in stone, tapestry, and furnishings.

In avoiding direct discourse, the Symbolists had dreamed of a universal language comprehensible to the cultural elite of their time, and the common denominator of that language was the almost automatic response to myth allusions. Mallarmé, in his role as both pre- and postsymbolist, envisaged the dangers of routine comprehension of mythical connotations and circumvented the normal allusion to avoid the danger of conventionalization. He thereby drew attention to the need to revise and transfer the initial automatic response. The desire to readjust the so-called universal language becomes in him not an effort to achieve simultaneous and unilateral identification of allusions in all the languages of the world, but to establish universally a new approach to the reading of poetry in the process of which the reference becomes the common denominator not merely of significations. It is expected that the personal adjustment to the reference will be made in an infinite spectrum of deviations and elaborations. "I am inventing a language which must necessarily surge out of a new poiesis which I can define in these two words: *to paint not the thing but the effect it produces*" is the way he explains the writing of *Hérodiade* in a letter to his friend, Henri Cazalis, in October 1864 (1440).

Hérodiade is not the mother of Salome in Mallarmé's text, nor is the naming a misnomer for Salome. The name represents an inheritance of a dangerous nature, the power of sustaining a pregnant stillness, of turning apparent purity into evil—a dimension of time, short but momentous, that was to be used effectively in post-Symbolist drama and in the poetry of Valéry, Yeats, and Rilke—what I will henceforth refer to as the "turning point," a moment that lies outside the chronological measurement of time, whose *effect* can create or alter phenomena. What lurks in the matrix of the transmitted heritage of Herod is much more awe-inspiring than any one crime Salome can commit, no matter how repulsive. Or to transfer the implication to another register, that of the process of creative writing, the unexpressed potential of the gestating work of art is illimitable in relation to any single product of writing that can emerge. This same potential of the unsaid or unrealized is the power of the message we shall observe in Rilke's sonnet of the fig tree.

The third device for evasion is of course the one we know most about in relation to Mallarmé's work: the return to verbal denotation, the freeing of the baggage of connotations grown stale. Charles Chassé's *Les Clés de Mallarmé*[5] has done much to show the apparent use Mallarmé made of Littré's etymological dictionary. When Roland Barthes talked of a methodology resembling the peeling of an onion to get to the core of meaning in literary analysis (see *Le Degré zéro de l'écriture*), he could not have had Mallarmé in mind. Mallarmé's writing is devoid of rhetoric. Not only did he peel the French language to its essential meaning, freeing it from the lexical encumbrances of time and place, but once the stark meanings were faced he then attacked the semantic functions to which usage had subjected them. So the words, like diamonds exposed to dust, were polished back to their luminous original quality to register not the accepted reality but a fictitious one in the blockage that he produced in the movement toward normal associations.

Further study of the relationship of Littré to Mallarmé's use of language has led me to the realization that Littré's[6] pursuits

---

[5] See Charles Chassé, *Les Clefs de Mallarmé* (Paris, 1954).

[6] See Emile Littré, *Histoire de la langue française* (Paris, 1886), conclusion of the introduction.

of the origin of signification, largely influenced by the discoveries of German linguists such as Friederich Diez, had a corollary even more important to poets: that denotation at origin, and successive connotations could be concorded in polysemic meaning *synchronically* to achieve comprehensive signification, paralleling "geological formations" of linguistic fossils and stratifications, as Sainte-Beuve restated Littré's observations.[7] As we examine Mallarmé's system of arbitrary substitutions, we note that knowledge of etymology went deeper than the retrieval of earlier meanings of significations, but more fundamentally to the general permissibility of altered meanings: a nostalgia for the primitive practice of polyvalence stirs Mallarmé to the possibility of using language in its several registers simultaneously, creating a potential for a mystery that might replace that of the scriptures or oracles of old. This maneuver, exercised with care, is the foundation of his notion of fiction.

With these three forms of deformation of the elements with which poetry is normally made, *Hérodiade* becomes a fiction of poetic vision.

There is no doubt that whether Mallarmé intended to create a theatrical piece or an opera or even a dance, the effect he wanted to produce was visual and representationally objective, devoid of the autointerpretive act so often associated in his time with both the poet and the novelist appropriating this archetype.

Although the first discourse of the Overture (not published until after the death of the author) is by the Nurse, emblematic of the standard human voice that recounts experience and emits thought, she is, as we soon find out, the one who directs the response of the reader to the setting. She is a mediator guiding the eye of the reader. In translating George Cox's *The Ancient Gods*, Mallarmé was to espouse the mythograph's belief that all myth and folklore originated in interpretations of the movements of the sun, stars, and earth; all legends were embodi-

[7] See Sainte-Beuve, *Premiers Lundis*, vol. 3 (Paris, 1858), 121

ments in an animated aspect of cosmology. Here, then, the real actor is not the Nurse but the Dawn, which we are made to follow like the eye of a camera into a place full of evidences of devastation:

> Abolie, et son aile affreuse dans les larmes
> Du bassin, aboli, qui mire les alarmes,
> Des ors nus fustigeant l'espace cramoisi,
> Une Aurore a, plumage héraldique, choisi
> Notre tour cinéraire et sacrificatrice,
> Lourde tombe qu'a fuie un bel oiseau, caprice
> Solitaire d'aurore au vain plumage noir . . .
> Ah! des pays déchus et tristes le manoir!

> [Abolished and her fearful wing in the tears
> Of the basin, abolished, which stares at the alarms
> Of nude golds flagellating the scarlet-hued space,
> A Dawn has, armorial plumage, chosen
> This our tower, ash-scattered and sacrificial,
> Oppressive tomb fled by a beautiful bird, lone
> Caprice of dawn with shadowy, black plumage . . .
> Ah! of lands fallen and mournful the dwelling place!]

(translated by Donald Friedman)

Let me note the features of this impermeable passage. In a self-referential play of imagery, it conveys the notion of decrepitude that unites a failed sunrise with a deteriorating castle. The key work is "abolished," in its feminine ending referring to the dawn ("aurore"), and in its masculine ending two lines later referring to the dilapidated moat ("bassin"), which used to guard the castle from the peril of invasion. The dawn depicted as an incapacitated bird drops its tears ("larmes") in the dried-up moat that no longer forewarns of danger, and the dawn's uncertain rays pass through a red and uncertain morning sky heralding doom and sparking in the crumbling structure gold spots that evoke past glories of the fallen domain. The red sky of morning, a proverbial sailor's warning of impending storm, is the first danger signal; in the stillness of a prestorm atmosphere we are first taken to the exterior approaches of the interior space separated from the exterior world by a window designated not by the common word for a glass opening, which would have been "fenêtre," but by one that we are accustomed to using in religious connotation—"vitrail"—in French, a separate lexical identity, whereas in English "stained-glass window" is a mere modification of the common garden variety and does not immediately conjure a holy object. The first word of the text, "abolie," which becomes a frequent lexical choice for Mallarmé, is an element of the deconstruction of reality. This unusual use of French syntax puts the reader's normal verbal associations immediately in a state of suspension. It is not clear who or what is abolished in the feminine past-participle form of the verb until the fourth line, although the repetition of the same past-participle in the masculine in the second line, aligned with the masculine "bassin," has had the effect of obliterating the topography through which we made our way to the spot illuminated. "Vitrail" gives a sense of the process of the destructive effect of a red sunrise, vulnerable itself, and spreading vulnerability upon organic entities among which only hard metals resist in their barren resilience to the changing atmospheric pressures. A red, tearful aurora contaminates space and alights on a fortress associated with words signifying destruction and decomposition, such as "tomb," "mausoleum," "incinerator," and "dead star," which presage doom and are arbitrarily ominous since the choice of aurora is capricious as it seeks a complicity among elements of fire, air, earth, and water in their choice of this particular place for an imminent sacrifice. "Crime! stake! ancient aurora! punishment" bespeak a drama that, if cast in movement and time, would take reams of paper to transcribe and, even on the stage, an hour or two to represent. For Mallarmé four words suffice to tell us the story of Hérodiade. The reader is spared the mimetic dimensions necessary to transmit into normal reading time the imagined state of the poet. In the use of "ancienne" in connection with "aurore" Mallarmé's support of the initial "abolie" is double-tiered: it contains the mythological context of a legend revisited on us and the perennial character of sunrise that is no longer relevant to his new use of the old phenomena in either their physical or their mythical functions. By contamination, the sense of crime and punishment must be equally banished or abolished as we enter an inner space that has established its bonds in terms of both its legendary and its cosmological filiations.

The ray of crimson—we must note that such an obvious word as "red" will not enter Mallarmé's lexicon—has penetrated the chamber, and the reader glides in on its path. The effect of "abolie" is continued through "éteinte" [extinguished] and "neigeux jadis," where the adverb indicating a long forsaken past is used as a noun (he was to create the same disturbing effect with "aujourd'hui" in his sonnet "Le vierge, le vivace et le bel aujourd'hui") and is associated with snow, which is a potent cover-up of reality and also, for one as steeped in French literature as Mallarmé, an appropriation from Villon's "Où sont les neiges d'antan?" where Villon recalled beautiful ladies of a historical past, thought to be so remote as to become legendary. We also know from the first section that autumn's fiery colors had yielded passage to a more fiery conflagration of a burning dawn. So the retreat into abolished time is becoming deeper as we advance into the setting and its artificial climate. The next grimoire/glyphe is woven into tapestry—also an act of abolition, for is there anything more useless than shrouded eyes of sibyls whose usual function is to look into the future but who, in this situation, are woven into a future that is long past?

The next passage, in which the Nurse seems to absorb the material texture of the tapestry as well as the prophetic function of the sibyls, is grammatically too intricate to promote a sequence of meanings. But whatever meanings the reader's efforts extricate from the sibylic words, by its very nature the discourse prohibits unilateral meaning. The reader is freed of any meanings the author may have had in mind. The morphologically obscure passage demonstrates that contrary to the repeated declaration that *Hérodiade* is a poem of absence, the elements of a vanished past have a functional presence. The topography of the tapestry is transferring the investiture of its qualities into the garment worn by a nurse like the passage of its effects into the room on the wings of an aroma that spills over its regret. The silenced voice (auditory absence) assumes the communicative power of the olfactory sense that has the power to be prevailingly present in its invisibility, having the resilience of flowers that refuse to lose or close their petals with the coming of night. The effect of immanence, prevalence, and resistance is masterfully suggested by the unlikely and unexpected alliance of fragile aroma with the hard metal "aroma of cold ores."

The lines of the passage of a historic past into a fictitious present could command a whole book of commentary, so intricate are the qualifiers between substantives and the repetitions of possessive connectors that, instead of soldering appropriation, confound the relationships. The reader is put into the process of weaving the tapestry himself whereby the visionary capacity of a past and buried eye and a past frail finger leaves its residual effect on all the inert present, thus making the absence of a time long past a possible presence as an agent.

In all this concrete set of denotations, there is not a single abstract word or idea. There is no rarefaction to suggest ambiguity or generalization. The key sentence repeats the initial image that englobes cosmic, animal, and human elements in a conjunction suggesting tragic impasse. And all that was emblematic of an aggressive war-oriented past is in a state of *concrete* extinction: "orfevrerie éteinte," represented in the "useless folds" of the tapestry. The reader's eye is made to wander from the lifeless tapestry to the empty bed, the waxed-down candle replaced by a feeble dawn dragging its wings in a pool of tears.

The rest of the Overture prepares the closure of an era—the millennium, the absence of the ruler, the power of prophecy of the old finger whose warning goes unheeded. And we are made to see the impact of a sunrise that is, in the fictitious climate the reader has embraced, semantically a twilight. It is captured in the image of a candle burning out or a star whose present light is the luminous absence of a constellation long dead.

The presence of Hérodiade is designated by her empty bed, in which she has left the purity of a creaseless sheet.

Critical references to "Scène," the second part of *Hérodiade* as published in the Pléiade edition, have been somewhat more numerous than those to the Overture, but they also bear the mark of embarrassing and understandable inconclusiveness on the part of the interpreter. Such interpretations of the hermetic text lean heavily on the biographical situation of the text and to references to other texts or, as a last resort, to Freudian interpretations equating the mystery that Hérodiade feels to intimations of unconscious forces. In a sense, the last part, "Cantique de Saint Jean," which verbally is perhaps the most cryptic of all, has to the reader an easier referential access because of what is *not* in the poem rather than what *is* in it. The beheading of Saint Jean is such a collective reference that substitutions of the common knowledge to the language of Mallarmé are readily possible, as is the recognition of the parallelism between the rise and fall of the sun and the rise and fall of the head of the saint.

But actually, verbal explanations of any part of the poem are counterproductive activities on the part of the reader in the light of one of the basic theories of the poet—that is, his desire to find a new language that would imitate the other arts in conveying ambivalent meaning and shrouding the ideological meanings of poetry, so that it becomes no more accessible to conceptual explanation than are music or visual art. Instead, the reader must assume a world of fiction such as when placed in the presence of a musical composition or a painting of landscape that remains ever green, of faces that do not wrinkle, of flowers that never fade.

39

The musical impressionism of the Overture defies conceptual sequence and must be received as a line of music and its concurrent harmonies.

If reception of Mallarmé's poetry is to be anything but exegesis or a blanket dismissal as "obscure," then his intentions must be taken into account: "Verse must thus be not a composition of words, but of intentions" (1440). And the intention is to take from music its power to impress and evoke rather than to transmit thought, from dance the fusion of the creator with the object of the creation, and from painting indisputable transformation of the mimetic into fictional and permanent existence. Mallarmé *intends* to use the qualities of all three of these arts in the writing of his poem, which is conceived in turn as dance, opera, and fresco, but always falls back into poetry; it is rejected as poem, edited endlessly, never released as a completed work, the intention never quite fulfilled, the process relentless.

Impressionism dominates the Overture, and, like the function inherent in overtures, it contains the comprehensiveness of motives, elaborated in the next parts of the poem, which were no doubt intended to be much longer and more elaborate than they turned out to be. Ominous in its effects, did it not suggest a climax in brutality and destruction? On another tier, it is also suggestive in terms of the arts of a "fin de siècle," of what Mallarmé characterized elsewhere as an "interrègne"—a gap in the continuity in the progress of the arts, paralleled in the political emblem of Herod as a break in the command.

The "Scène," with its emulation of operatic recitative and with a certain outside resemblance to the Nurse's scene in Shakespeare's *Romeo and Juliet*, focuses on the ambiguity of action on the part of the principal persona. The Nurse, in her inquisitiveness, assumes the position of the spectator to some succinct and impending drama; she verbalizes the probe into the mystery of human behavior in the impatient expectation of the loved one. But here the parallel stops. For whereas in Shakespeare the Nurse's inquiry is into very basic and universal

human behavior, here the dialogue involves the dichotomy between the human and the desire to be nonhuman. The central
image is *hair*, organically the human element most resilient to
putrefaction, and metonymically representative of the beauty
of woman (human) and transformed by its possessor into
something nonhuman, gold, metal, untouchable, eventually elevated to the level of a meteor. Behind the will to transform the
human into something inhuman is the intention of the poet to
be other than what he is: man into woman, historical situation
into legendary, poet into archeologist, his writing into sculp-
ture, his communication into gesture, the stillness of the physical environment into movement, his folio into mirror, the mirror into deep well; if the poet, who characteristically avoids the
word "poet" in virtually all his writing and wanted to find
something other than his self-portrait in his writings, were simply retreating into his subconscious, as our Freud-oriented
contemporary commentators would have us believe, he would
indeed be sinking into the quicksand of the ego.[8]

"On ne peut le comprendre d'une façon tout à fait complète
que si l'on se rend compte que le poète est en communion avec
les profondeurs de l'inconscient" [One cannot understand him
completely unless one realizes that the poet is in communion
with the depths of the unconscious]—whatever that means!
But the case of Mallarmé is quite the opposite. He intends to
escape from the human self and, not believing in sainthood, is
faced with the tragic dilemma of the agnostic. Rejecting the
human, he makes Hérodiade say: "But who would touch me,
respected as I am by the lions / Besides I want nothing human,
sculptured as I am"—and yet at the same time hating the azure
and having nothing else to cling to!

The legendary dance of Hérodiade is here transformed into
a gradual fixation into immobility; as eyes become jewels, darkness willed to be a permanent atmospheric condition, she
awaits a metamorphosis that will distance ineffective dreams,

---

[8] Cf. Charles Mauron, *Introduction à la psychoanalyse de Mallarmé*.

and turn useless flesh into cold—but enduring—stone. Let us take note of Mallarmé's many returning references to stone, which result in the verbal tombstones he will create in memory of his dead friends in his poems called "Tombeaux." Stone was destined to become an important image in the fiction of the poet, recurring in both Rilke and Stevens.

Many years later, Jacques Maritain, the Thomist theologian of the twentieth century and an astute literary critic as well, was to discuss in *Frontiers of Poetry*[9] the dilemma of the modern poet. He feared that the poet's spirituality leading to an aesthetic manifestation might be mistaken by him and by his readers for an ascetic experience. But the crisis of Mallarmé and the most sensitive of the symbolist poets after him was caused precisely by the desire to avoid that confusion. They strove in the wake of Mallarmé to find means of expression containing that passage out of the strictly human, without transcendence into theological experience. *Hérodiade* is the cornerstone of that confrontation. And taken in that light, the severance from life, the closing of the windows and blowing out of the candle, paralleled by the descent into a hinterland between life and non-life, the recognition of the vanity of "human" mystery, the nudity of flesh without future, all lead to the worship of art as the only alternative to death, but art must recoil from the human as Hérodiade recoils when the Nurse tries to touch her hair; art can survive for Mallarmé and his followers to the degree that it can detach itself from the mimetic and create its own fiction, as an ontology separate from theological perceptions.

Although it is not clear when the "Cantique de Saint Jean" was actually written in the chronological composition of *Hérodiade*, and although it was not published in Mallarmé's lifetime, the logic of its presentation after the "Scène" is obvious in light of the struggle that the totality of the concept represents. The decapitation of Saint Jean is as normal as the closing

[9] See Jacques Maritain, *Frontières de la Poésie* (Paris, 1935), trans. Joseph W. Evans under the title *Art and Scholasticism, and the Frontiers of Poetry* (New York, 1962).

of the shutters in "Scène" and the extinguishing of the candle in *Igitur*.

To reach the "Cantique," we pass from intention to premonition, and finally to realization in the most radical rupture with the past. If in "Scène" Hérodiade rejects human procreation, in Saint Jean the rejection extends to the theological. If the movement of the decapitation is compared to the movements of the rise and fall of the sun, that may be its visible structure indeed. But if Hérodiade is basically Mallarmé, the poet, then so is Saint Jean, in spite of the dramatic presentation of its persona. The saint is fictitious like every other character in Mallarmé's work, be it derived from classical or Hebraic mythology. Saint Jean is Mallarmé in the process of self-immolation; we witness the process of his severance, expressed in the instrument of the "faux" [scythe], from the interrelationships with the body. Mallarmé views the decapitation not as a death, in terms of his artistic life, but as "vols triomphants" this time, opting for the independence of the creative process, a new baptism: "illuminated" qualifies "head" four stanzas earlier as the fact is fulfilled according to the principle "which elected me," the severance making a new kind of salvation possible. Of the three parts, the "Cantique" is the least somber, the fall being equated with a strange kind of triumph, the orphic return from darkness into illumination in the kind of relief from frustration that alone saves the artist-persona of all time from suicide. We have in the case of Mallarmé the answer to the Nurse's question to Hérodiade: "Madame, allez-vous donc mourir?" ["Madam, are you then intent on dying?"]. The answer is no, for, like Orpheus, the poet returns from death to lead an existence better explained in his next and more complete statement of the function of the poet in *L'Après-midi d'un faune*.

L'Après-midi d'un faune has been more pondered over and commentated on than *Hérodiade*. The brilliant Sicilian sun under which its setting is cast appears to illuminate the intricacies of a style as syntactically structured as in *Hérodiade* and as abstruse in reality. But perhaps the very popularity of the leg-

43

end seems to make the meaning more accessible to the readers of his and all time. As usual, Mallarmé's escape from chronological time plunges him into the common legendary heritage. In this case the source is even more specific. As the Salome legend was in very current usage, so was the story of Pan. It is generally agreed that the particular variation on the legend was furnished to Mallarmé by Théodore de Banville and reinforced by his having seen a painting by Boucher in London, entitled *Pan and Syrinx*, depicting two nymphs lying side by side at a river's edge with Pan observing them from afar. The legendary commentary, backing this representation, is that Syrinx—one of the nymphs—was pursued by satyrs, asked the assistance of naiads, was submerged by them in the waters over which they ruled, and was thus hidden. When Pan, the satyr, tried to seize the submerging nymph, he found only a bunch of reeds, whereupon he cut them up into pipes of unequal length and made an instrument in memory of the Syrinx and called it by her name.

Combining the memory of the writing of Banville, the painting of Boucher, and the collective knowledge of the legend, Mallarmé's scenario runs like this: the Faun discovers the nymphs and wants to love both of them, but they escape. Having paid his respect to legend, Mallarmé gets to the crux of things. The problem with Mallarmé's Pan is that he does not know whether he really saw the nymphs or was dreaming. He awakens and tries to reconstruct from memory either the reality or the dream, both equally ineffable and unsubstantial. To achieve the reconstruction he tries the powers of music and of intoxication to evoke the reality or the illusion, only to realize that it really does not matter whether the imprint of the experience is real, evidenced by the marks of teeth in his flesh, or a dream; what matters is the fact that he can give the lived/dreamed experience a permanent reality through the work of art by creating his own fiction as Boucher, the painter, did before him, and which Debussy was to do in his musical interpretation of the theme.

But here we are neither dealing with an appropriation of artistic techniques foreign to the art of writing poetry, as Mallarmé attempted in *Hérodiade*, nor simply proving the triumph of art over life, but introducing the reader into the struggle and process of creation.

The struggle is between the physical and the aesthetic, between the narration of the ephemeral experience—the creation of a verbal image beyond both reality and dream. Since they are both taken to be passing experiences, the reconstruction of the terms of the fiction of his art "le souffle artificiel" [the artificial breath] is achieved by a series of word substitutions, all avoiding the obvious denotations of "poet."

> Suffoquant de chaleurs le matin frais s'il lutte
> Ne murmure point d'eau que ne verse ma flute
> Au bosquet arrosé d'accords; et le seul vent
> Qu'il disperse le son dans une pluie aride,
> Hors des deux tuyaux prompt à s'exhaler avant
> Qu'il disperse le son dans une pluie aride,
> C'est, â l'horizon pas remué d'une ride,
> Le visible et serein souffle artificiel
> De l'inspiration qui regagne le ciel.
>
> [Stifling with warmth the cool forenoon if it strives,
> No water purls not poured forth by my flute,
> Upon the grove watered with chords; and the sole wind
> Outside the twin pipes, quick to be exhaled before
> It scatters the sound in an arid downpour,
> Is, on the horizon, not stirred by a ripple,
> The artificial breath, serene and visible,
> Of inspiration, climbing homeward to the sky.
> Of inspiration, which regains the sky.]

(translated by Donald Friedman)

The reader is allowed to witness the artist's skill not only in restoring the memory or dream but in watching the Faun/Artist—and again, as in *Hérodiade*, Mallarmé is his own central character—revising it, correcting it, recasting it, and finally breathing new substance into it, whereupon he can regain serenity and fall asleep, again to dream, but this time of what he has put into the work of art. Nowhere as in this poem is the process of fictionalizing reality so richly demonstrated in its modulations and struggles.

In the very first line, the intention is quite clear: "These nymphs, I want to perpetuate them." It could of course mean perpetuate the human experience, make it last in the impact of its sensuality. But being privy to Mallarmé's language, we know that "perpetuate" is one of those words of evasion, or substitution for artistic creation. The next lines have already depersonalized the nymphs, and we have left only the metonymy of the *glow*-effect, drenched, as it were, with sleep. Immediately there arises the doubt as to the nature of the vision: was it real or a dream? Looking longingly at the real woods, he knows that his first response to the retrospective experience— in the *afternoon* evoking something that happened in the morning—was the futile triumph of "la faute idéale de roses." The fault or default inherent in the rose is at the very heart of the default of reality. It must be noted that if Mallarmé was thinking of *rose* in terms of the individual rose category rather than some other flower, he would have said, "la faute idéale *des* roses," as if roses had a particular weakness not to be found in other flowers. But the omission of the article turns the rose into a *quality* comparable to that of "incarnat" earlier in the poem and becomes the rose quality, which will be remembered and elaborated by Rilke under other forms, such as that quality which is at the same time the beauty and perishability of reality, even in its loveliest form. "Idéale" is referring to its purity only as it is identified in human terms, purity to be violated if it is to become triumphant in art.

So the process of turning reality or dream based on reality into the poet's fiction ends in rape here as it does in decapitation in *Hérodiade*. How the supreme sensual leap into a double rape of maidens in the context of a legendary ecology becomes

46

the triumph of the poet over what is for him an impossible reality, is immediately keyed into the language of his fiction. We have had "perpetuate." It will be followed by "réflechissons" (the first-person plural takes the reader on as an accomplice), "les femmes dont tu gloses" bringing a rather unusual substitute for writing: "glose," a word having few connotations behind its denotation, "tes sens fabuleux"—senses have taken on a new function, that of creating a fable, and the whole ecological setting is under the control of the musician/writer as the "artificial breath" of inspiration rises to the sky. The important word is "artificial," as opposed to the natural, and the "ciel," although already possessing the double meaning in French of sky/heaven has here that of the physical sky overpowered by the divinity of the art-sky, untouched by cloud or wind (freed from the natural attributes, atmospheres) and "visible" even as the tangible countenance of artifice.

The rest of the poem is an alternation between the act of creating—"contez," "refleurir," "regonflons des souvenirs"—and sharing the process of creating with the reader, the ecstasy and frustration of one who is looking for "le la." Here again he borrows from music the tuning-up process that is a prelude to the harmonizing of the orchestra. At the same time he is comparing the creative power of language to the art of painting. The intoxication, via the grapes, is a lens to the fictitious vision and the willed construction.

> Tâche donc, instrument des fuites, ô maligne
> Syrinx, de refleurir aux lacs où tu m'attends
> Moi, de ma rumeur fier, je vais parler longtemps
> Des déesses; et par d'idôlâtres peintures
> A l'ombre enlever encore des ceintures;
> Ainsi, quand des raisins j'ai sucé la clarté,
> Pour bannir un regret par ma feinte écarté,
> Rieur, j'élève au ciel d'été la grappe vide
> Et, soufflant dans ses peaux lumineuses, avide
> D'ivresse, jusqu'au soir je regarde au travers.

[Try then, instrument of my flights, oh maliciously playful / Syrinx, to reflower at lakesides where you await me. / As for me, proud of the sounds I make, I will be talking for a long time to come / of the goddesses; and in idolatrous paintings / continue to remove belts from their shadow figures. / And so, when I have sucked away the glow of the grapes, / to banish a regret distanced by my pretense, / laughingly I lift to the sky the empty cluster /and, blowing into its luminous skins, avidly / seeking intoxication I look through them until dusk.]

Better than in any of his theoretical writings Mallarmé prescribes here his notion of poetry; these lines contain the process and the product of the process simultaneously. Syrinx, invoked, becomes both the subject and the object of the work of art as it plots the work of art; in his perception of the essential synchronization of all art, Mallarmé first denotes a musical instrument, the syrinx, and then evokes painting—and all the time the reader knows that he is really talking about writing. "Idolatrous paintings" suggest worship of what is godlike. All this in concrete language! The attitude of the artist is one of defiance, "tant pis," if he lost the real thing; he can re-create it better than real! Impudence, mockery—"maligne," "fier," "rieur" all suggest irreverence of god-associated creativity now taken on and expressed by two natural images that are destroyed in the very act of being conveyed. To deflower what is absent: "A leur ombre enlever encore des ceintures" and to empty the natural fruit and infuse into the skin, which is the shell (parallel to the "ombre" image) his own essence, creating his own pleasure in what is nothingness, holding up the nothingness to the sky, using the old word in its new connotation as he enjoys what only the artist's eye can create in imperishable dimensions. The self-excitation that his own words create leads him from the capture of half-goddesses to the supreme goddess herself (Venus), to the forbidden fruit for the savoring of which punishment may be due, but, shrugging off the implications of his verbal transgression, he falls exhausted into sleep as after a sexual frenzy. He has perpetuated his nymphs not in a single enjoyment, as mortals are wont to do, but in double intensity on the eternal afternoon in which art, in the framework of absolute time, takes him outside of the human competition or of even the divine, and of the limited consequences of human voluptuousness. Without trying to formulate any philosophical statement, he expresses his will to preserve in his own dictated eternity the ephemeral human experience of a morning of ecstasy by means of very concrete and obsessively lingering images in an afternoon in which he re-creates them. In them is revealed the poet's action to overcome temporal limitations as well as the spatial ones of the interiors of limited dimensions that encompassed his constricted life pattern.

Whether expressing that quest for purity which destroys life and its standard salvations, or the quest for desire as it swarms and bursts out of our skin, Mallarmé's overreach of the human is a created fiction that destroys what it asserts and, in escaping the "faute idéale de roses," inevitably falls into traps of his own making. He has verbalized these self-inflicted impasses in his "Le vierge, le vivace et le bel aujourd'hui" in the image of the swan trapped in ice, conceding its impossible flights, his position reminiscent of that of the live soldier in Baudelaire's "La Cloche fêlée," who lies at the bottom of a heap of dead soldiers, the ever-present demon of the artist whose achievements always fall short of the effort of his intentions.

Indeed, in the case of Mallarmé and of those to be viewed in his wake, the artist triumphant over reality is not a triumphant artist. A series of "pyrrhic victories" lead eventually to the somber poems of the *Tombeaux* and the final *Un Coup de dés jamais n'abolira le hasard*. If a poem such as *L'Après-midi* intimates the victory of art over human frustration, the artist is not thereby freed of frustration as an artist. The battle against annihilation becomes a double one—that of the simple human, first, but also that of the artist. We know the three stages of the Orpheus myth: his defiance of the gods and entry into the forbidden realm, followed by his immolation, which in turn is followed

49

by his reconstructed terms of the song and its unifying domination of all. The same pattern is followed in the myth of Osiris in the Egyptian counterpart. But the poetic Orpheus of latter-day symbolism reflects the shaken faith in the immortality of art itself.

If Mallarmé vies with nature in creating his fictitious world, he knows as he ultimately states it in *Un Coup de dés jamais n'abolira le hasard* that it is a "false abode" which quickly evaporates into the fog of the cosmos; it is a futile attempt to delimit a space in the infinite. The fiction of the poet does not guarantee the survival of art over human mortality; even "the hope of the corridor" before the eternal darkness, which he halfheartedly promised Théophile Gautier in his memorial to him, "Toast funèbre," is grim—as are all his *Tombeaux*. All leave a preponderant image of hard, impervious rock, a quiet obscure disaster and irreversible oblivion. He offers "his empty cup" as he encloses the poet *and* his glory with "the thick iron of the tomb's doors." "Magnificence" and "abolition" are words that Mallarmé uses in serial recurrence, as if he were composing varying musical phrases that return to reinforce the effect of the contradiction that is intrinsic to the destiny of human efforts at creation. If a glimmer of confidence in the survival of the work remained for Mallarmé, it was lodged in the mitigating effect of a questioned negative: "Is there of this destiny nothing that remains, no?" ("Toast funèbre").

In his final struggle with the unconcerned universe, the casting of the dice, which is perceived as an infinitesimal and faint atmospheric disturbance, does not in the least alter the neutrality of the abyss. "Perhaps"—which is featured at one point in the nonlinear disposition of the page in *Un Coup de dés*—is wishful thinking. Much more overwhelming are the clusters of images that spell out the poet's fiction as "an empty act." "Close the shutters" and "blow out the candle," which are earlier images of Mallarmé's *Hérodiade* and *Igitur*, are here summed up in the total capitulation. The last throw of the dice when we are almost sure of the odds against us makes of the *Coup de dés* the apocalyptic saga of the nineteenth century. The theme of the cosmic annihilation comes back in Yeats's "The Second Coming" and in other "wasteland" poetry of the postsymbolists.

If in much of his poetry Mallarmé has freed his reader from the writer's meaning,[10] if he has absolved words from their known commitments to previous relationships, a whole new *écriture* emerges at the end, giving words a prismatic expression, making them a vehicle for the suppression of all eloquence. Each word has contaminating seepage that permeates the poet's world of fiction. The ultimate concession that Mallarmé's followers will make in this direction is to admit that this "other world" can be no more than an interspace, and the poet no more than an intermediary: ephebe, angel, mime, ever fallible even in his ultimate fiction, creating a typology that was to become familiar in the poetry of the last decades of the anthropocentric universe.

[10] Malcolm Bowie, in *Mallarmé and the Art of Being Difficult* (Cambridge, 1978), has made the very relevant observation that "difficulty" in Mallarmé is a positive factor.

51

Valéry and the Imagined Self

V ALÉRY IS the most evolved, polished practitioner of the poetic discourse in the decades of his literary eminence among the
inheritors of the Symbolist mode. Both his poetics and his theories place Valéry quite close to the dictums of Mallarmé.

Like Mallarmé, he believes that poetry must be architectural
and premeditated. He sees in Mallarmé's treatment of literature
"the most audacious and continuous attempt ever made to sur-
mount what I will call the naive intuition in literature" (1.620).
Much of the filtered theories of symbolism as implemented by
Mallarmé rather than by the *cénacle* that surrounded him are
appropriated *in principle* by the poet most closely meriting the
title of direct heir of poetic and intellectual stature. The bond
is given a concrete character by the fact that their personal as
well as intellectual closeness reached a climax when Valéry was
the one to whom Mallarmé returned the proofs of *Un Coup de
dés* for publication in *Cosmopolis* the last year of his life (1.625).
He believes that Mallarmé understood language as if he were
its inventor (1.688). He acknowledges "the enormous influence acquired over a very small number by the difficult, perfect
poet . . . in whom we found the extreme rigor of the dogma of
art" (1.674). He approves and carries a few steps further the
notion of the artifices that convey the world of the poet as distinct from the representation of the natural world. This assumption is ever-present in his critical writings.

Without using the word "fiction" in the Mallarméan sense,
Valéry conveys the meaning of that word by the frequent use of
the word "artifice" and, moving yet farther from mimesis and
truth, suggests a deception of the reader by using the word
"mensonge." In fact, he defines the imagination thus: "L'imagination significative est une tricherie affective" [The imagina-

tion that signifies is an affective trickery]. Also like Mallarmé, he believes that the resources of language are endless and that words cannot be limited in their capacity to convey meaning: "Il n'y a pas de vrai sens d'un texte" [A text has no true meaning] ("Variété," 1.1307). Being Socratic and more historically inclined than Mallarmé, he universalizes the attribute by approximating what the modern poet does with the sense of "fable" in the ancients. The last line of his study of Edgar Allan Poe, entitled "Au sujet d'Eureka," is "Au commencement était la Fable. Elle y sera toujours" [In the beginning was the Fable,and so it will ever be] (1.867).

The associations Mallarmé made with other arts that had shunned representation and were therefore models for the poet to follow were Music and Dance; Valéry extends the list to include Architecture, which he particularly favors. He binds these three to the creative power as perceived by the poet, that of *construction*: geometric, consciously contrived or connived, yet avoiding specific perception of reality, all three evolving structures artificial to nature's system. Dance is not walking, Music does not represent nature's noises, Architecture transforms inert materials into composition that links the useful (reality) with the aesthetic (imaginary). "Or, de tous les actes, le plus complet est celui de construire" [Consequently, the most complete of all acts is that of constructing] (2.143).

In the *Philosophie de la Danse* the distancing of art from reality has several phases: a space-time relationship different from that of life, and "artificial somnambulism," a semblance of noneffort that is the result of "a principle of artifices." Valéry had read Mallarmé's perceptions of the Dance and he felt that "Mallarmé avait épuisé le sujet en tant qu'il appartient à la littérature" [Mallarmé had exhausted the subject as far as literature is concerned] (2.1407). Yet Mallarmé's provocative statements were to trigger responses from Valéry and through Valéry, as will be seen, to Rilke. Most important of these observations was of course the sense of the near-perfect amalgamation of the concrete and the abstract, expressed in the notion that a dancer is not a woman who dances; she is a metaphor, an ambiguous one inviting decipherings—and in its very physicality the Dance becomes ironically "fictive and momentary," that is, free of time and space. The hieroglyphic character of the Dance observed by Mallarmé is transformed into the metaphor of a flame by Valéry, a power without a tangible form—a fact he asserts in one of his Socratic dialogues. His fictitious Socrates says that the dancing figure has more power to alter the nature of things than any philosophical speculations: "assez puissant pour altérer plus profondément la nature des choses que jamais l'esprit dans ses speculations et dans ses songes n'y parvint" [powerful enough to alter more profoundly the nature of things than ever the mind succeeded in its speculations and its dreams] (2.174). Dance is destructive, as is flame—destructive of reality. The spirit of lie (fiction) and Music, also considered "lie," possess and save the human consciousness from "la nulle réalité" (2.171). Metaphor becomes metamorphosis in Valéry as the Dance takes on a more dynamic form, although it is harder to discern in Valéry's poetic writings the structural imitations of dance—no one has been able to my knowledge to do as yet a choreographic presentation of *La Jeune Parque*, as has been done many times of *The Afternoon of a Faun!*

But the supremacy of Architecture is most elaborately discussed in Valéry's article on *Eupalinos*. Music and Architecture fill the poet's "knowledge and space with artificial truths" (2.104) and that is why the poet discerns a profound kinship with these two arts. He talks of Architecture in relation to Music because he is comparing functions and not structures. There we have the basic assumption of what is the power of survival of the symbolist aesthetic: the creation of what Valéry terms "a divine ambiguity," which in the Dance consisted of the orchestration of the movements of the body; the same figuration and purity of execution occurs in Music and Architecture through very conscious calculation. The simulation of these arts by the poet is to achieve the same sense of ease and spontaneity through the conscious uses of language which achieve, in their very deliberation, the sense of facility and creative fallacy that are mere illusions. Thereby they reach that otherness possible through the creative coordination of the senses of sight and hearing.

> Mais la Musique et l'Architecture nous font penser à tout autre chose qu'elles-mêmes; elles sont au milieu de ce monde, comme les monuments d'un autre monde; ou bien comme les exemples, çà et là disséminés, d'une structure et d'une durée qui ne sont pas celles des êres mais celles des formes et des lois. Elles semblent vouées à nous rappeler directement—l'une, la formation de l'univers, l'autre, son ordre et sa stabilité.

> [But Music and Architecture make us think of things entirely different from themselves; they are in the middle of this world, like the monuments of another world; or else like the examples, dispersed here and there, of a structure and of a duration which are not those of beings but of forms and laws. They seem bent on reminding us directly—one of the formation of the universe, the other of its order and stability.] (2.105)

He aspires to that ideal in his own art: "to borrow the least possible from natural objects, and to imitate the least possible" (2.106) common attributes of the two arts, with the implication that they might reach and be realized in the art of poetry as well. In his treatise on *L'Arbre* Valéry also makes a distinction between truth and nature, putting truth closer to art than to nature: "Il est certain (et il est étrange, en effet), que le vrai ne puisse nous être connu que par l'emploi de beaucoup d'artifices. Rien de moins naturel!" [It is certain (and it is in fact strange) that truth is revealed to us only through the use of a lot of artifice. Nothing is less natural!] (2.189). Of course, the best-known of his treatises elaborating his search for system is his *Introduction à la Méthode de Léonardo da Vinci*, in which he perceived da Vinci as the artist prototype who best succeeded in relating calculation (the scientific) with the creation of the affective state essential to art.

Not only in theory but in the appropriation of the great themes, Valéry sticks close to Mallarmé: the need to take the reader into the throes of process as part of the function of the poet, the ability to establish a series of interferences in the path of direct communication, and principally that of mythic creatures, repersonalized by the poet. He colonizes, as we shall note, the sites of the in-between world. If through the *Igitur* vision Mallarmé focused on the in-between of being and nonbeing—which indeed was to become the problem of Orpheus more visibly and successfully developed by Rilke—here we have in Valéry the in-between of self and its reflection, or the problem of Narcissus—"cette tremblante, frêle, et pieuse distance / Entre moi-même et l'onde" [That trembling, frail, and pious distance / between myself and the water] (1.130). He searches also for the interval between consciousness and unconsciousness, the terrain explored in *La Jeune Parque*, aptly identified in an earlier title as "Iles."

One of his most poetic delineations of the interspace comes in his *Eupalinos*, which he puts in the mouth of Socrates—the description of space as the undistinguishable frontier/nonfrontier between land and sea: "Cette frontière de Neptune et de la Terre, toujours disputée par les divinités rivales" [That frontier of Neptune and the Earth, always disputed by rival divinities] (2.117). We can read the overtones of the poet ready to capture: "ce que rejette la mer, ce que la terre ne sait pas retenir, les épaves énigmatiques" [what the sea rejects, what the earth cannot retain, that enigmatic flotsam] (1.117). Of the pool of natural images used by the Symbolists and postsymbolists as personal re-creations, we find the rose, water, and tree predominant in the poetry—the rose elevated beyond its "faute idéale," the water turned away from its function as reflector, and the tree becoming enigmatic because its visible stature is not an indication of its potential for growth; thus a parallel is established in the course of the dialogue *L'Arbre* between Tityre and Lucrèce in which the stark, concrete reality of the visible tree is transformed into an apprehensive ambiguity of potential, calculated in its internal time machine but mysterious to the beholder of its outside appearance. "La vie en lui calcule, exhausse une structure, et rayonne son nombre par les branches et leurs brins, et chaque brin sa feuille, aux points mêmes marqués dans le naissant futur . . ." [Life calculates inside of it, erects within it a structure, and radiates its number by the branches and their twigs, and each blade its leaf marked in its very tip for a future being born . . .] (2.195).

What happens to the animal kingdom, stylized into swans and unusual birds in the vocabulary of the symbolists? The swan reference is slim and infrequent in Valéry. The interesting animal is the serpent, whose role has the calculated ambiguity of a symbol in the important poetic writings.

But where Valéry can be best seriated with postsymbolists and, by the same token, differentiated from them is in his major poems. The theme of *L'Après-midi d'un faune* is replayed and transposed and finally recomposed in the Narcissus poems, where the interplay between nymphs and their charmer is altered to reach conclusions other than those of Mallarmé; *La Jeune Parque* takes up the leitmotif of *Hérodiade* contemplating the self with outcomes different from the ones in *Hérodiade*, and Valéry's preoccupation with the passage from life into death is crystallized in what is perhaps his best poem, *Le Cimetière marin*, which leads the poet to a triumph over the philosophy of symbolism in the very process of using that *écriture* against itself.

Whereas the connection between Mallarmé and Valéry seems on the surface to be the most natural and complete in view of theory evoked and historical records that ascertain contact-influence, other factors enter into Valéry's development and the alteration of the intellectual climate, moving from Nietzsche to Freud, as well as a sudden critical participation in the problems of aesthetics that inevitably and interestingly transform the symbolist vision for him. Principally, "the cult of the self" and the notion of "poésie pure" infiltrate the interstices of Symbolism and leave very significant imprints on his writing at least equal to if not greater than Mallarmé's notion of the supreme poetic act.

Maurice Barrès popularized the cult of the Ego in the late nineteenth century, and André Gide, who was a friend of both Barrés and Valéry, became the intermediary. The philosophical probing into the self as the only fountain of unmitigated truth of which man could be certain, was given psychological support through the introduction of Freud's ideas, if not his texts directly (very tardily translated into French), concerning the unconscious. The hearsay mystery, possible of being unraveled through the interpretation of dreams and the study of insanity, caused reactions among the literati. The most spectacular of these responses are known through the novelists of the period and through the spectacular adherences of the surrealists. They are differently and more subtly evident in Valéry's *Narcisse* and *La Jeune Parque* poems and have drawn less critical attention in relation to these texts.

As earlier noted, Mallarmé had conjectured his intercourse with the reader on two possible levels: objectification of preexisting inner states and interiorization of a perceived and commonly recognized reality. Although Mallarmé made use of both systems in his poetic writings, his most successful method and the one most closely illustrative of his theory of the value of the work of art was the objectification system. Neither *Hérodiade* nor the *Faun* are chance figures caught within the range of vision and used as sources of perception of the self. The very fact that Mallarmé thought of his two great poems as *dramatic* presentations demonstrates the importance of the process of objectification of self-expression and the universalization not simply of the Ego but of the artifact. As a hermeneutical device it has an ultimately independent existence from the purposes of the creator of the work. The oft-quoted line from *Crise de vers* that posits the disappearance of the elocutionary self into the poem (and not *from* the poem, as the phrase is sometimes interpreted), is superbly illustrated in those two great poems.

The process is quite different in Valéry. The image of Narcissus and La Jeune Parque, which might be considered his answers to Pan and Hérodiade, are chosen as *vehicles* with the a priori objective of the exploration of the Ego. They are not projections into an independent world of fiction but pretexts for interiorizations, descents into self-perception, and they reveal the process of abstraction of the concrete images connected with the myths.

This abstraction of the concrete conforms with the notion of pure poetry, rampant in the 1910s in France, which would have purified symbolism of its newfound liberty of language had l'Abbé Brémond's theory pushed its way beyond the frontiers of the French language. The fact that it was confined to a national movement made it possible for a more pristine passage of Mallarmé's sense of language and of the symbol into territories of poetic fermentation beyond the French tradition.

The notion of "pure poetry" caught Valéry, however. Here are words that are limpid, that ring like a pure bell, that convey their ambiguity through their connotative generalizations rather than through perplexing denotations. Valéry's themes generally fall into verbal expression that scintillates in its non-contamination, very often making of his world an ideological, platonic locus rather than the concrete albeit fictitious one of Mallarmé.

Already in their perception of language there is a clear distinction. Valéry tells us that language is an instrument, a tool; "le langage est un instrument, un outil, ou plutôt une collection d'outils et d'opérations formée par la pratique et asservie à elle" [Language is an instrument, a tool, or rather a collection of tools and operations formed through practice and subservient to it] ("Propos sur la poésie," 2.1365). We saw earlier how Mallarmé, on the contrary, perceives language as a body of flesh and bone carrying a life of its own and significations beyond those intended by the poet, who can persuade but not control its ultimate target.

Valéry's purification of language leads to ideas. Although he tells us that he is sharing a process with the readers, they are in fact led to the product, to witness its realization rather than the stages of fictionalization. The blurred vision has become clear, not different. There is crystallization and ultimately a philosophical conclusion.

One of the pitfalls of Symbolism that Mallarmé avoided, but in which most of his international successors were caught at some time or other, was philosophical poetry. Even in his use of the Hamlet leitmotif—"the bourn from which no traveler returns," concretized in *Igitur*—he does not say it in so many words. It creates the effect of one caught in that perception, haunted by it and eventually delivered of it.

Valéry's passages through the nether lands of in-between existence are fraught with battles with philosophical discourse. In Mallarmé's poem we saw Pan's operations, whereby Pan created his own nymphs and went into a sleep to savor them, whereas in Valéry's *Fragments du Narcisse* we have the statement instead of the sensation; we share the *idea* rather than the *state*:

> Que nulle vierge enfant échappée au satyre,
> Nulle! aux fuites habiles, aux chutes sans émoi
> Nulle des nymphes, nulle amie ne m'attire
> Comme tu fais sur l'onde, inépuisable Moi.

[Let no virgin who has managed to escape the Satyr, / none capable of clever flights, undisturbed by falls, / no nymphs, no friend attract me / as you do on the water, oh my inexhaustible Self.] (1.126)

In like fashion, when *La Jeune Parque* proposes the great theme of Hérodiade—that of waiting—instead of the terror of Hérodiade's impending doom we find la Jeune Parque making the serenely philosophical generalization: "Tout peut naître ici-bas d'une attente infinie" [Everything can be born here on earth from an infinite awaiting] (1.98).

A closer look at these poems reveals these two types of important deviations from the Mallarmé writing. The trigger to the creative process in Valéry's case is indeed an exterior inspiration to the poem, as in the case of Mallarmé's contemplating the painting of Boucher or seeing interpretations of the Salome legend by artists and poets of his time. In the case of Narcissus, the Pléiade edition of Gide's *Traité de Narcisse* gives the explicit circumstances under which both Gide and his friend Valéry encountered, in a cemetery of Montpellier, the tombstone of a certain Narcissa—presumably the burial site of the daughter of Edward Young, the English poet of the eighteenth century who lived for a while in France and is better known there than in England for his pre-Romantic, gothic prose-poems, *Night Thoughts*. His daughter's real name, Eliza, had been romanticized into Narcissa, and the association that both Gide and Valéry made with the myth of Narcissus had more to do with their own cultural background and preoccupations with the cult of self than with any associations with the daughter of the poet. What is clear is that the association did occur, arousing the imagination of both writers to develop the theme of Narcissus simultaneously with the *Traité* appearing in 1892 (it was completed in 1891) and Valéry's *Fragments* surfacing in 1891, with correspondence between Gide and Valéry during the gestation period. Both pregnant with the idea of Narcissa, one produced his work in prose, the other in verse. Gide's was straightforward, direct in its communication, and terminal; Valéry's was indirect, destructive in its interpretation of the legends, and recurred in several texts. Neither makes any allusions in the work itself to the object triggering the initial inspiration.

This, then, is a distinct departure from Mallarmé's procedure, for Mallarmé keeps contact with the painterly postures of the Faun as if he were describing the mythical figure, and having caught the subject from the painting of two nymphs and a faun who is eyeing both of them at once, he awakens to the fact of his own suppressed eroticism. In recasting the myth perceived beyond its representation in the painting, he covers the reality of his own sensual deficiency in creating a fiction, this time a poem or dance of opera, which both drowns and solves his own personal problem. In the case of both Gide and Valéry, the circumstances under which their imagination was triggered have no relevance at all to the writing except to remind them of the myth of Narcissus in its abstract state, and to draw modern conclusions from it in terms of their personal lives through an interiorization and abstraction, and meditation about the self. Interestingly, the two selves that emerge from the two personal preoccupations with the Ego are as different as were the personalities of Gide and Valéry.

Bypassing Gide, whose relationship with Valéry is in this instance merely circumstantial, the focus here is on the method, substance, and language in which Valéry differs from Mallarmé in the perception of a modern use of myth.

First of all, the assumption of the character of Narcissus does not turn Valéry's monologue into an indirect discourse, although it is full of ellipses. The basis on which he overreaches from the known myth to a new fable or fiction is the assumption that Narcissus sees more than his reflection in the water, and that he cannot love the nymphs because he is totally preoccupied with love of self. But the words "love" and "self" and the capitalized "Moi" have, in true symbolist fashion, deconstructed their expected meanings and assumed new ones. "Love" borders on knowledge, and "self" wavers in the in-between shadows of the conscious-unconscious awareness. Although Valéry, like his contemporaries, was much impressed with the studies of the unconscious, he was quite wary of anyone's power to reach the reality of the dream. Our concept of the dream, which is a past time in relation to our present consideration of it and has already lost something in the time-lag, is to our conscious awareness what the reflection in the water is to the reality of Narcissus in Valéry's perception. His lack of total recognition of self as he contemplates it is the metaphor of our inability to know our unconscious, even if we can name it as such.

Whereas Mallarmé, in the guise of the Faun, was evoking sensual experience in the re-creation of a dreamed or realized

63

sexual encounter, Valéry's Narcissus is pursuing an intellectual experience, culminating in an abstract reflection in the mind of the ambiguous being reflected in the water. It is interesting to note that there is, here as in Mallarmé's *Faun*, a reference to "morsure." This bite in the flesh of the Faun is concrete evidence of a sensual reality that Mallarmé is trying to transform into a fictional, perpetual one; in Valéry's Narcissus poems the "morsure" is that of a serpent—acute and fatal, one might presume, if the image were to be taken literally. But, on the contrary, the serpent here is an idealized image of wisdom, and therefore the "morsure" is like an injection of wisdom, the better to apprehend the nonparallel between body and soul, between this reality and—in order to avoid the theological one— what Valéry calls a second reality: "Le poison, mon poison, m'éclaire et se connaît" [The poison, my poison, enlightens me and knows what it is doing]. And the descent deepens and deepens "Jusque dans le replis de l'amour de soi-même" [All the way into the folds of self-love]. Although the "soi" gives a universal overtone to the statement, the reader has been drawn into what is no longer a monologue. The speaker is aware not of a theater audience but of a stream-of-consciousness discourse cut off from exterior disturbances. Mallarmé had said, "Ces nymphes, je les veux perpétuer." Through stylization he wanted to preserve them in their corporeal dimensions. Valéry is looking for essence:[1]

> Mais moi, Narcisse aimé, je ne suis curieux
> Que de ma seule essence
> Tout autre n'a pour moi qu'un coeur mystérieux,
> Tout autre n'est qu'absence.

[But I, beloved Narcissus, I am only curious / about my own essence. / All other being holds for me a mysterious heart, / all other is mere absence.] (1.128)

[1] In fact, in his article "Qual quelle: Les sources de Valéry," Jacques Derrida reduces all of Valéry to the search for sources: "sa soif de l'origine" (in *Marges* [Paris, 1972], 340).

Certainly the hair, the complexion, the belt, were not absences in Mallarmé's ecological setting. In Valéry there is evaporation and distancing through a process of abstraction that starves the vision's power to fictionalize and brings the poet closer to the philosopher.

But Valéry remains primarily a poet in his perception of love as knowledge and in his awareness of the scope of its physical impact. There is a temporality in the contemplative pose itself that guards Valéry from falling into theological ascesis. He remains in the poetic key even if his language returns to a classical harmony based on the dichotomous expression of the spiritual and material:

> Toi seul, ô mon cher corps,
> Je t'aime, unique objet qui me défends des morts.

[You alone, oh my dear body, / I love you, you alone protect me from the dead.] (1.129)

In the Narcissus poems, Valéry is struggling between two spaces—the forest and the fountain or source—each with its special attraction; at the moment of the poem, he is in neither of these spaces, but characteristically symbolist in the ambiguity of his position between the two, trying to comprehend what separates the one from the other. In that precarious interspace he tackles the Faun problem and the Igitur/Orpheus problem, those two basic centers of the poetic meditation of the Symbolists. As he contemplates the possibility of passage from the corporeal to the shadow, he reviews his options: the transgression of the Faun (mortal) in capturing divinity, and the sensation of passage from material sensations to imagined transformations into otherness. What he does not consider, through oversight or intention, is the possibility of return from descent (Orpheus) or that of the preservation of the experience in the fictitious immortality of the work of art. Out of a work rich in the artistry of the experience, the intention appears to be existential rather than a triumphant statement about art, as it was in the case of Mallarmé and many other postsymbolists. "The bourn from which no traveler returns" is indeed that, but the attraction to it is not one fraught with emotional disarray or mental depression; rather, it is in step with the epistemological search that French poetry had undertaken ever since Baudelaire's "Plonger. . . . Au fond de l'Inconnu, pour trouver du *nouveau*" [to plunge . . . into the pit of the unknown to find something new]. Here the "nouveau" is not exterior to oneself; it is, if anything, a deepening of the sense of self that Valéry's adept use of reflexives makes dramatically cogent: "celui qui s'approche de soi" [he who approaches himself]. Valéry desperately needs an extra word within the antithesis created between the flesh and the spirit that would be the arbiter and the ultimate witness of the passage, so he uses in a special and modern way the word "âme," giving it neither a spiritual nor a corporeal sense, but one denoted as an observer comprehending the dual desires and capacities of the human condition.

The two areas that encompass the totality of man's desire for knowledge and that become the battlefields of his struggle are metaphorically represented by the forest/trees (the concrete reality of man) and the water with all the elements that people it, including physical flowers and reeds, and its divinities, the nymphs. Unlike the situation in *L'Après-midi d'un faune*, where Mallarmé deplores the escape of the nymphs from his clutches, Valéry fears being captured by the attraction of the nymphs—for contact with immortals means corporeal annihilation for him. He tells them to stand off, to sleep! "Votre sommeil importe à mon enchantement" [Your sleep is important to my enchantment] (1.122). The nymphs have come to compete with his attraction to himself, and to suggest the very physicality of his infatuation with self, Valéry conducts a virtual verbal masturbation in the life/death struggle in which shadow fights substance, and is likely to overcome substance because of its kinship with and perfection of that substance in its shadow state. The juxtaposition of the ineffable with the material, of the ephemeral with what endures, was quite tolerable to the symbolist optic.

What makes the present situation curious and more sophisticated than most such symbolist imagery is that the accepted connotations of "ephemeral" and "durable" are interchanged as the total ambiguity looms in the marriage of the two qualities in "éphémère immortel—plus parfait que moi-même" [ephemerally immortal—more perfect than myself] (1.125). Nonexistent spirit is more ephemeral than mortal existence, and yet more perfect in its quality of absence. Driven by the search for essential perfection as a resource of the self viewable only in the shadow, it casts the poem in a long conversation with self in the realization that the price for the ultimate knowledge of self is the annihilation of the seeker of the knowledge in the very process of attaining that knowledge. It is neither a Faun who will disdain divinity by creating his own powerful illusion in art, nor a semi-deity Orpheus who will challenge the nonreturnability of man from the depths and risk destruction through faith in resurrection. It is a new Adam on the verge of annihilation who contemplates with philosophical serenity his self-immolation without hope of being recuperable as he meditates on the brink—I say on the brink, because the poem does not proceed to its logical termination. There is the struggle of the first part, the approaching of the forbidden terrain, "Un désir sur soi-même essayer son pouvoir" [A desire to try one's power over one's self]. But the plunge does not occur. There is no parallel here to the "Je vais voir l'ombre que tu devins" of Mallarmé. Valéry tells us that he was tempted to end the poem with a convocation of the abolished image of Narcissus but did not do it. He abruptly terminated with "Brise Narcisse." And because of its conceptually unresolved status, he called the text "cet ensemble imparfait" [this imperfect assemblage].

But this reading of Narcissus is not intended to present a Faustian struggle between lust and knowledge; Valéry's dilemma is couched in purely poetic terms. The vision is one of passage from the body to the shadow and its resolution, left ambiguous. The resulting absolution into an image that retains the essence when the substance has been devoured juxtaposes not simply the contradictory inclinations of the poet but evokes verbally the contradictory character of the two sites.

There is a language of destruction and annihilation ironically associated with *purity*, coupled with the notion of fatality: "Que je déplore ton éclat fatal et pur / Si mollement de moi, fontaine environnée" [How I deplore your fatal and pure luster, / fountain so gently surrounded by myself] (1.124). "Pure" is a word in Valéry's vocabulary that corresponds to "abolie" in Mallarmé's particular lexical use of the word. It characterizes Valéry's notion of the noncorporeal without the implied advantages of the transcendental. Obsessively the word "pure" in its frightening connotation recurs throughout the poems from *Narcisse parle* to *Fragments*, always associated with the water and its funereal implications. "Tu (eau) consommes en toi leur perte solennelle" [you absorb their solemn loss] (1.126).

The sites of life are evoked in the context of trees, foliage, and forest: "De toute une forêt qui se consume, ceinte / Et prise dans l'azur vivant par tant d'oiseaux" [of a whole forest that is spent, besieged, and captured in living daylight by so many birds / those huge and shaking bodies that struggle mouth to mouth] (1.128), and in the more perfect verbal coordination of life-elements exemplified in "Tout un sombre trésor de fables et de feuilles" [an entire and somber treasure of fables and foliage] (1.126), man's creation in coalition with nature's. Or again: "Ces grands corps chancelants qui luttent bouche à bouche" (1.127), as the struggle of the one becomes that of the human condition as a whole, and then falls back on the individual's fate.

The choice that the poet has between the two forces is also metaphorically envisioned: "Tout m'appelle et m'enchaîne à la chair lumineuse / Que m'oppose des eaux la paix vertigineuse" [Everything calls me and chains me to the luminous flesh which confronts me with the vertiginous peace of the waters] (1.124). It is to be noted that light is the quality of the human, associated with the flesh, and elsewhere with the power of the sun, which keeps alive the human and loses its hold over it only in the crepuscular phase of the day when the moon favors the waters. The struggle between life and death is also the struggle between the sun and the moon. And water qualified as "vertigineuse" is here centered on its meaning of precipice that draws toward destruction. Sometimes the struggle is evoked by metonymic devices related to the human but taking opposite significations because of the dislocation of one of the terms: "Entre ce front si pur et ma lourde mémoire" [Between this brow so pure and my heavily laden memory] (1.125). The pure brow is that of the image of Narcissus in the water, and although the poet is drawn almost by a pull of gravity toward that more perfect knowledge of his own essence, the weight of living memories effects a balance that saves him momentarily from the destructive pull.

The opposition of the two types of language suggests the tension of the descent into annihilation of an Orpheus who cannot return, and the temporary respite granted by the forces of life. In Valéry's work, unlike Mallarmé's, there is an absence of the compensatory forces of the artist's powers over both domains, which are neither overtly asserted nor inherently confirmed. Ironically, the struggle does not consist of a perilous attraction of the void, against the corporeal life, but is motivated by the vision of the greater beauty of the shadow over substance. The shadow beguiles and entraps the mortal, and in the ultimate union with him annihilates what it promised and disappears:

> Penche-toi . . . Baise-toi, Tremble de tout ton être
> L'insaisissable amour que tu me vins promettre
> Passe, et dans un frisson, brise Narcisse, et fuit . . .

[Bend, kiss me, tremble with all your being. / The elusive love that you have promised me, / passes, and in a shudder, crushes Narcissus and flees . . .] (1.130; final lines of the poem).

What detracts from the symbolist climate is the survival in Valéry's style of the heritage of both Classicism and Romanticism. He has not abandoned the classical structure of the verse with the regularity of the antithetical imagery, its apostrophes, and invocations. To suggest ambiguity, he resorts to images of absence rather than to some subtler substitution devices and concrete discontinuities of the symbolist discourse: in his juxtaposition of the clarity of the void with images of the *angst* of man, an ambivalent state in symbolist poets, his cognizance is not stated but self-explanatory as he proceeds through the forest in which he sows his symbols.

A lingering Romanticism is evident in the language of Valéry, which preserves the animism of an anthropocentric universe—whereas the symbolists of the latter period, in the wake of Mallarmé, were abandoning it. Instead, in Valéry's verse, the rock laughs, water is sad, the moon is perfidious, the glow is tender, and the tree cries.

The epistemological factor in poetic creativity is more extensively satisfied in *La Jeune Parque* than elsewhere in Valéry's writings. The search into the multilayered self, this time not in the depth of a pool but in the remote islands of awareness, is a personalized Freudian experience for him. In fact, he had been tempted to call his work "Psyche" but desisted out of deference to his writer friend, Pierre Louys, who had just used that title. In discussing the title actually used, commentators have stressed the "jeune" of the name as "young" in reference to the known legendary elderly sisters, the three fates who mythologically spun out Man's fate. However, "jeune" has another meaning more appropriate to Valéry's purpose: it also means "new"—and, in terms of the intellectual excitement of his time, psychology was the *new* interpreter of human destiny.[2] At the time he was writing the long poem (between 1913 and 1917) he had the acute sense that something in the world he had

[2] Modern psychocriticism points out the various negative allusions to Freud and psychoanalysis in Valéry. He himself acknowledges this dislike in his essay "Propos sur la poésie."

known was in danger of a catastrophe and that French was a dying language. As in much of the poetry derived from Symbolism, which destroyed so many of the subjects previously considered legitimate to poetry, the expressions qualifying the human condition were retained and Valéry's visionary propensities heightened. Even as we shall note in Yeats, Valéry was, during the writing of *La Jeune Parque*, very much concerned with the fate of humanity. He himself points out in his notes that this is a wartime poem, although there is not a single overtly circumstantial reference to the Great War.

This is the time when Apollinaire, in the thick of the conflagration, was writing *Calligrammes* and approximating verbal explosions with those of modern artillery warfare. It was a time of patriotic poetry, such as Charles Peguy's and Paul Claudel's. There is not an *apparent* reference, I say, to all of this circumstantial data; but if the allusions are not apparent there is indeed a very deep relationship in the *sense of peril* that is the primary power of the poem, a sense of uncertainty even more compelling than the sense of apocalypse in *Hérodiade*, over the future of Man, his fate seeming to go out of all control. Can the *new* Parca come to salvage the human species? Will the greater knowledge of personality advance us toward control of society as it moves inexorably toward the precipice? Like Mallarmé, Valéry escapes from time, one might say, but again the legend is rewritten—as in Mallarmé's case—to adapt to disquietudes that overreach the specific period and create poetic states with which universal identification is possible.[3]

To return to the "new" Parca, why does Valéry—like Mallarmé before him—identify with a female character rather than with one of his own sex? Perhaps because the sense of peril is not only an intellectual awareness but an intuitive one, and intuition as a source of cognition was also very much in the air as

---

[3] A renewed invocation of the Parca can be noted during World War II in André Breton's *Fata Morgana*.

Bergson became for that generation what Swedenborg had been for the Romantics and early Symbolists. Intuition was associated with the female in the legendary practice and in "modern" psychological studies of Valéry's time. Certainly there is a struggle in the poem between intelligence and intuition as the poet plunges deeper and deeper into another of those interspaces, this time between consciousness (intelligence) and the unconscious. Actually, commentators have been made uncomfortable by the passage of identity from male to female as the poem progresses. That unease can be dissipated and replaced by a sense of unity if "La Jeune Parque" can be perceived as the same type of androgenous character as Balzac's Seraphita-Seraphitus. As the "Moi" of the speaking voice in the poem moves from masculine to feminine qualifiers and back, it simulates man's ever-ambiguous position in testing his visionary powers through the double entry into the unknown via the forces of reason and intuition. This is parallel in its oscillation to a musical modulation that takes the poet from nocturnal darkness into dawn, back into darkness, and again into an ultimate light.

If there was ever an exercise in fiction, it is the construction of the character of the "New Parca," a figment of Valéry's imagination no more identifiable with the legend than was the Hérodiade of Mallarmé.

So much has already been critically asserted about the difficulty of the poem, its impermeability to any form of deciphering, that any attempt at exegesis would be based on arbitrary premises. In any case, it would not serve this inquiry into the creative process associable with the enduring impact of the symbolist mode. In looking at some of the details, therefore, in the text itself, what matters to this reader is the evidence of the practice of the theory as it emanates from the language, rather than the reduction of the text to conceptual statements that can possibly be derived from it. The principal concern is to note how and how much Valéry is in fact able to guard himself from falling into philosophical statement, dealing as he does with a theme so susceptible to philosophical treatment:

> Qui pleure là, sinon le vent simple, à cette heure
> Seule, avec diamants extrêmes? Mais qui pleure,
> Si proche de moi-même au moment de pleurer?

[Who is crying there, if not merely the wind, at this hour / alone, with the brightest diamonds? But who is crying, / so close to myself at the moment of crying?] (1.97)

"Pleure" and "Proche" are the two words in the first three lines essential to the texture of the poem, suggesting the profound distress and its integrality with the life process of the poet. It is to be elaborated (like a melody and its variations) in the lines that follow, with "distraitement docile" suggesting a trapped condition, and "larmes," "coeur brisé," "amèrement," "plainte," and "resserrement" all supportive variables of "pleure"; and all the elements of the universe are allied in the state that is summed up in the word "désastre" that comes as a final chord in the first stage of the recitative. "La houle" (water) participates with "gorges de roche" and "feuille effacée" (earth) and "ciel inconnu" (air), all joining in a *cluster*, which is the meaning most appropriate for "grappe," creating a confluence of forces evoking a sense of disaster. That the concern is intuitive is evidenced by the fact that Valéry is questioning "îles." The image is so important to him that he had at some point had in mind the possibility of using it as the title of the poem. In poetry the "island" image qualifies in general the remoteness of a geographical space, identified with the concept of the unknown. When Mallarmé in "Brise marine" wants to lift anchor and escape, to express the totality of his desired landscape, he identifies an unidentifiable space beyond even the space of islands, "sans îlots." In Valéry, ironically and effectively, and in keeping with the psychological concepts of the time, the islands of remoteness are situated in his/her breast, and the word "sein" recurring throughout the poem is in its physicality more associable with geography than the semantically watered-down anatomical designation "coeur." "Heart" had assumed too connotative a usage to suggest the ambiguity of what is at once close and yet remote, which was the comprehensive meaning of the psyche as understood by people at the threshold of the era of psychology.

The next stanza makes the normal inquiry into astrology to explain the disquietude of the poet's state as he wakes up in the middle of the night with the blurred memory of the serpent's bite, in that suspended moment in time when the past of the dream is questioned as a portent by the awakened dreamer. And suddenly we are in the same dual perception as in the Narcissus poems: that of the identification of the viewer with the viewed, the prober (the conscious) and the probed (the unconscious): "Je me voyais me voir, sinueuse et dorais / De regards en regards, mes profondes forêts" [I saw myself sinuously seeing me and gilded my deep forests as my glance caught them] (1.97).

Here explication can occur exclusively in terms of symbolist substitution techniques: "or" here and in the Narcissus poems is a substitute for "light," thence the verb "dorer" would mean "threw light." In his viewing of his inner, intuitive self, the poet is trying to throw light on his "profondes forêts"—another displacement of geographical language into physiological. The Swedenborgian forest of symbols (later he talks also of "inner deserts") familiar to Valéry's readers is now identified with the newer psychological use of the word "symbol" in the interpretation of dreams:

> Quel repli de désirs, sa traîne! . . . Quel désordre
> De trésors s'arrachant à mon avidité,
> Et quelle sombre soif de la limpidité!

[What sinuosity of desires, its train! . . . What treasures / in disorder that shake off my greed, / and in a limpid state how foreboding is my thirst!] (1.97)

The next three lines bring another set of substitutes we already recognize in Valéry's code: "soif de la limpidité," where he questions whether his proclivity for impending disaster is to be explained by an unconscious thirst for purity ("limpide" is a substitution for "purity," which, as we have seen in *Narcisse*, is intimately associable with water, which equates with annihilation). Is the disaster-fear based in a death wish? That is what Valéry would have asked as a philosopher or a psychologist. In what follows there is a struggle on a much more intricate level between the forces of the conscious self-concern of the poet, "Moi, je veille," and the forces, intuitive, unconscious, revelatory and at the same time elusive of the dream, "légère mort," resisting "souveraine," rising to "à la toute-puissante altitude," only to be reversed into the antithesis of eyelashes blindly illuminated: "Quel éclat sur mes cils aveuglément dorés." Both "cil" and "paupière" suggest closed eyes (in sleep), parts of the eye structure that, when open, do not draw attention to themselves. The poet's intelligence is laid low ("opprimé") by the treasure of the night—that is, dream—and from the altitudes (of clear vision) he is dragged into another paradoxical state where he fumbles ("à tâtons"), that of "Ténèbres d'or" combining darkness with light, or, to be more explicit, again in terms of the great wave of enthusiasm for the interpretation of dreams: in the very obscurity of the remembered dream-vision lies the knowledge of the self.

His struggle with the temptation and resistance to the unconscious is associated with the sense of individual liberty over the uncontrollable (or fate). It is envisioned in terms of a strong body, nakedly prevailing to maintain the continuity of the mortal race. And then, Valéry arrives in more simple expression to the great leitmotif of *Hérodiade* as his ambivalence is injected into the struggle between will and its ultimate annihilation: "Je regrette à demi cette vaine puissance" [I half regret this vain power] (1.100).

There is a sense of chase in which the poet is tempted into adventure like Orpheus, "mon oeil noir est le seuil d'infernales demeures" suggesting the interiority of this particular concept of hell. He catalogs the ambiguities and enigmas of that shadow space located between the physical world and the total sense of self: "Entre la rose et moi, je la vois qui s'abrite." He is hunter and hunted alternatively, as much a captive of earth as of the concept of heaven, "captif de mes réseaux d'azur," and a free spirit, "déchirant departs des archipels superbes," all the while wishing to sever his bonds with his divided self. Long passages develop Mallarmé's theme of "la faute idéale de roses" as the symbol of his three-leveled mortality.

As dawn returns in the semblance of a bare arm, "Je te revois," the dream takes the metaphor of a voyage with all the references of a remembered sea journey: bark, sail, fishermen, foam, marine sounds, wave, and "écueil." Restored to clarity, he finds himself not altogether free. The disappearing shadow (dream) leaves him sensually susceptible to new desires associated with the memory of past ones: "Me découvre vermeille à de nouveaux désirs." Divine powers associated again in a metonymic suggestion of land and sea to something quite physical rather than spiritual. "Divinités par la rose [earth] et le sel [sea]" [Divinities suggestive of earth, suggestive of sea] (1.106).

The next invocation of the Psyche as Iles is less apprehensive, more explicit (in the structure of a classical apostrophe), more like an ode in praise of the Fates of ancient time: "marveilleuses Parques." The last part of the poem suggests the supremacy of the lucid "I" only in the disdain of the "nuances" of fate in *life* as opposed to the unnuanced certainty of death. This verbalization has philosophical tones, avoided in large measure by the poet through a process of emptying concrete images of their known substances, a verbal evaporation—"un aromatique avenir de fumée"—in the journey toward *essence*. The passages that follow are couched in funereal language reminiscent of Igitur's entombment among the ashes of his ancestors. The descent that was not quite completed in *Fragments du Narcisse* is simulated here in the construction of a verbal state of absence. "Forme-toi cette absence," clearly in keeping with Valéry's sense of construction, is carried out even in the context of destruction.

But the finale of the poem is a surprise to the reader as it is to the writer in the throes of writing: "Vains adieux si je vis." Inadvertently his presumed voyage into death was only that preexperience with death that is contained in the mortal's power to induce sleep. The popular association of the conquest of the subconscious with an experience into the total annihilation of the conscious knowledge of the fundamental life force is only one step on this side of the orphic experience, and so the Orpheus of the infernal descent into self, like the legendary Orpheus, returns, "Doux et puissant retour du délice de naître," and in the last two stanzas a heroic ascending sign, unfamiliar to the Symbolists, emerges. It has recourse to both the philosophical and poetic discourse, and restores the intelligent Ego to a faith in the renewal of knowledge in a primal, physical state. The return of this awareness is coupled with the key word "or," referring to both physical and intellectual light.

We have here, then, a poem of process, mitigated by exterior and interior fears, all the exterior globality of sites serving to communicate the interior conflicts and the self-analysis of a rational man flirting with the irrational and thereby discovering a new frontier in the in-between sites of the poetic fiction.

In his poetically most accomplished and unified text on the subject of mortality, *Le Cimetière Marin*, Valéry summarizes, or rather synthesizes, both the advances he has made in his *écriture* and the compromises he has made in his life philosophy. In a network of verbal associations between the ineffable and the concrete, the interior architecture parallels the exterior—"l'édifice dans l'âme." The correspondences are sustained with extraordinary precision. Valéry consolidates his stoical optimism of postwar "new beginnings" in his post-apocalyptic "Il faut tenter de vivre," in a philosophical conciliation between an inbred nihilism and a newly assumed vitalism that was echoing everywhere around him after the Armistice. He projects the alliance in the vision of a cemetery replete with the shades of the dead, but visited by birds—a site for the dead and the living at the same time, "où picoraient des focs." He also achieves a postsymbolist style that joins the forces of classical poetic discourse with the symbolist evocatory devices, creating a more compacted structure, yet invigorating, through this alternating current, the lights that had grown faint . . .

It is clear that without Valéry's example as an intermediary, neither Jorge Guillén nor Rilke would have discerned the possibilities of compromise between symbolist evanescence and the constructive spirit that was resurging in the arts of the twentieth century.

Rilke and the Unseizable

FROM THE POINT of view of poetic language, Rainer Maria Rilke is uneven as a poet although he is a superbly poetic being. Too often his commentators, bent on studying his poetic language, experience the same pitfall as Rilke himself: they express Rilke's philosophy instead of discovering how the philosophy takes poetic form and to what extent Rilke himself slips from time to time from poetry containing a philosophy into philosophy couched in poetic rhetoric. Perhaps if we could banish Nietzsche and Heidegger from his frame of reference, we would reach the heart of Rilke's poetics more directly. The fault lies equally with Rilke and his critics, virtually all of whom have been admirers.[1] But before I presume to become the only commentator finding fault with Rilke, I should hasten to explain what I mean by "uneven." He has written in many styles and his poetic vision reaches us from various angles. His first contact with the French had familiarized him with the Parnassian aesthetics. From there he proceeded to an essential comprehension of Symbolism in the directly Mallarméan sense by bypassing the Symbolist *cénacle*'s technical preoccupations.

Rilke's identification with the nihilism of the decadent era gave him virtually the semblance of an archetype. The modes shifted from the ideals of concrete and brilliantly bold forms emanating from his first enthusiasm for Rodin, to the shady ambiguities that reflect the uncertainties of the human condition when the certainties had been undermined. And his obses-

---

[1] Since there are too many critical works on Rilke it would be an arbitrary choice to single out any special ones. The name of Rilke has also been often linked with that of Valéry, whom he called "another me." See Charles Dédeyan's four-volume study of Rilke's connections with France, *Rilke et la France* (Paris, 1961–63).

sive awareness of the intellectual upheavals of the time made the need to philosophize a more urgent priority than the need to chisel a new poetic language of his own in the manner of Rimbaud and Mallarmé, although he shared their intensity of poetic presence more wholly than most of their French contemporaries. Rilke had none of the linguistic preparation in German that the presymbolists had in French. That is why the encounter with Valéry was so crucial to his development as a poet; he recognized the compromise that Valéry had achieved in his *écriture* between the expression of philosophical propensities and the construction of a scale of imagery that identifies conceptual dilemmas without resolving them. As Monique Saint-Hélier reports in *A Rilke pour Noël*, "I was done, I was waiting, all my work was within. One day I read Valéry, and I knew that my waiting was at an end."[2]

Vacillating between the direct poetic communication of the German Romantics and Valéry's transpositions of symbolist idiom, Rilke's poetic communication is uneven. But when it achieves its goal, it is powerful beyond many a preconceived poiesis. When his *écriture*, developed in the process of writing the *Elegies* and the *Sonnets*,[3] succeeds in creating his own brand of poetic fiction, he develops an artificial universe closer to Mallarmé's than to Valéry's; but just as often, if not more so, he lapses into philosophic statement, inviting the kind of paraphrase and explication that I have earlier observed to be counterproductive in the comprehension of symbolist poetic experience. It is therefore to be noted from the start that discussion of Rilke in the context of this study will be confined to special instances of what from this point of view can be deemed "success" and pertinent to the symbolist principles functioning in the series of trials and achievements that originated with Mallarmé. This partial Rilke that may emerge from these pages will have to be complemented by other readings; and there are in-

[2] Monique St. Helier, *A Rilke pour Noël* (Berne, 1927), 21.

[3] The *Sonnets* are the most pertinent to the illustration of Rilke's appreciation of Mallarméan poetic theory.

numerable works of these by eminent critics that will give the reader a much more comprehensive view of one of the leading poets of the century than will be derived from these pages, which constitute a critical partita in the area of poetics.

The eminent Alsatian critic, Victor Hell,[4] in his perceptive and terse book on Rilke, observes that Rilke practices at times "l'art du raccourci," the art of the shortcut; this is indeed one of the elements of the *écriture* that aligns him with Mallarmé, Valéry, and Yeats in the use of the progressive ellipsis; the other pole of his symbolist style is the absence of closure in the poetic communication. Again, let me hasten to point out that this generalization, to be illustrated in what follows, does not apply to his total poetry, just as in Rimbaud's work the elliptic style of *Les Illuminations* does not apply to *Une Saison en Enfer*.

The established path of Rilke's education in poetry is traced from Romanticism to Parnassian aestheticism, and on to what has been called an ambiguous form of Christian mysticism, affected by his early readings of the Romanticists. His contact with the precise art of Rodin led him to his own descriptive poetry, and on to something more existential under the influence of Nietzsche and the waning Christianity of the era. What is significant here is that brief moment when "Bild" is replaced by "Figur," in Rilke's concept of the symbol, and when a figure in movement such as Angel, acrobat, dancer, falconer, horseman, and, particularly and most tellingly, Orpheus replaces the static notion suggested by a word-picture for "Bild," which is representative of an interpretable world of emotion, correspondences or allegory. It is at those moments when he expresses himself in terms of "Figur" that Rilke really reaches the complexity of the poetic sensibility of the symbolist sphere of fiction.

When in the First Elegy he chooses his particular Angel, he describes it as Rimbaud described his "génie" or "force"—by

---

[4] Victor Hell, *Rainer Maria Rilke, existence humaine et poésie orphique* (Paris, 1965).

81

contrasts and negations. We do not know what this angel is so much as we know what it is *not*. It is a being that is not comfortable in the *interpreted world*, "gedeuteten Welt." Where meaning is clear, the Angel does not belong. But the alternative to allegorical representation is to be neither meaningless nor distanced in holy evasiveness like the angels of Swedenborg. His figures are neither meaning-clear nor meaningless but simply outside the expected systems of interpretation. Rilke is not challenging Swedenborgian (Romantic) symbolism, but neither does he follow Baudelaire's less blatant, more devious manner of accepting correspondences and in the same breath rejecting the very spirit and objective for which they were meant.

Rilke's concise statement, not poetic in itself, opens up the empty spaces of potential meaning in the same manner as Mallarmé's "les vols qui n'ont pas fui." Instead of unflown flights—of the imagination—Rilke releases birds to "erweiterte Luft," that is, to unconceived spaces, open to an infinite range of conjectures on the part of the reader. Thereafter, he returns innumerable times to this vision of new arrangements of space; and through necessity he discovers the particular genius of the German language that can do and undo meaning with the same words, allow him to play with inner spaces ("Weltinnerraum"), between spaces ("Zwischenräume"), useless spaces ("unbrauchbaren Raum"), spaces of time ("Raüme der Zeit"), and spaces of being ("Raüme aus Wesen"), putting into movement these self-composing substantives that without being resolved into watertight metaphors can trigger the mental associations of the reader, just as in a serially structured musical composition the performer is given musical space for input! The linguistic play on space reflects those two qualities of Rilke's symbolist *écriture*: ellipsis and open-endedness.

It has often been mentioned that Rilke was obsessed with the notion of death for personal physical reasons and because the spirit of the times encouraged his own melancholy sense of mortality. As previously noted, the omnipresence of death was also a factor in the poetic vision of Mallarmé, who did not even share Rilke's ambivalent feelings about resurrection. These are self-evident facts that do not need repetition; however, in the case of both Mallarmé and Rilke it would be an error to try to explain the centrality of the images of death in terms of psychological obsessions from which the poet may have suffered. In the case of Rilke, as in that of Mallarmé, if we examine closely the works instead of their biographical backgrounds to justify their poetic vision of death, we can perceive that it is not death itself that is central but the *telling* of the experience beyond the conceptualizing of the event. Nowhere has the experience of death been poetisized as in Mallarmé's *Igitur* (which is in itself inappropriate to bring into a discussion of the heritage of symbolism since it did not surface into publication until the best of the postsymbolists had already made their mark), unless it is in Rilke's handling of the Orpheus theme in the *Sonnets*.

Mallarmé's descent by the ancestral stairs to the arena where furnishings shed their meanings and sound becomes shock, and his return from the underworld of his own inner space, are attempts to convey *verbally* rather than ideologically the sense of the passage from being to nonbeing and the return from nonbeing to being, in a strategy of verbal maneuvers. He was not thereby translating abstract notions into symbols; he used instead stark and single words harboring self-contained metaphors, which might act like light bulbs in the darkness of the reader's subconscious.

Without ever having been aware of *Igitur*, Rilke gives the same verbal and visual sense of being and not being. It has been noted by others that his Orpheus symbol is not simply an elegy for the forever lost Eurydice; but neither is it, as has been affirmed, simply an amalgamation of godlike forces with those of the natural world. Like the Angel, Orpheus is an ambiguous figure falling between the divine and the human. In the Third Sonnet Rilke says, "Ein Gott vermags," verbalizing what Mallarmé and Rimbaud dared not say openly although they sensed the demiurge in the poet; they chose a series of other substitutions for their concept of poet to erase the established meaning: Hérodiade, Faun, St. John the divine in the case of Mallarmé. In choosing Orpheus as his identity Rilke uses bolder strokes; he chooses a vulnerable figure but one who has a nonperishable instrument of communication—the lyre—which, like the syrinx of Mallarmé, is capable of overcoming both reality and the dream to reach other spheres of expression. The god victimized by other gods, tortured by them, will have the supreme experience to come back from death and to communicate the sense of human vulnerability and resilience not through words that express ideas but through those that simulate other forms of expression. These are the kind of modes of communication suggestive of music and calisthenics in their repetitive and accumulative structure freed from linguistic structure that has to combat immediate connotative assertions of words that might impede the desired suspension of meaning.

"Gesang ist Dasein," said Rilke in the Third Sonnet. And "Dasein" is unfortunately translated in English as "being." But Rilke was not talking about anything as finite and specific as *to be*. "Dasein" is *being there* or *becoming*, with all the fluctuations and ambiguities of progressive existence that opens on to non-existence as well, ever so much better expressed through the laws of gradual structuring in music and dance than through the immediate connotative assertions of words. But Rilke found extensions into a guarded transcendence within the Germanic word structure by using expressions such as "übersteht," "übertrifft," "über-schreitet" to create interaction between Earth and the stars. "A god can do it," but a poet (substituting for a god) fails to a certain extent. However, in his very failure he is closer to Orpheus, who also failed in not being able to bring back the message from the underworld—as Mallarmé felt a sense of failure when he called *Igitur* "la folie d'Elbehnon."

And so, song is that failed speech with all its ambiguities, the "Unsägliche" in Rilke's native tongue; to be aware of the potential of communication is the desire, implicit in the expression "spräche wäre, ohne sie spricht" [to create speech as if without speaking] in Part 2, Sonnet 20. The ambiguity of communication is expressed in this sonnet in a totally poetic manner without philosophical conceptualizations. To give the sense of the incommunicability of true poetic language in the context of prosody, Rilke suggests the inability to express distance between the visible and the inner intricacies of human relationships. Again in an abbreviated statement he creates the open character of meaning, the distance between designation and signification: "Alles ist weit und nirgends schliesst sich der Kreis" [Everything is far and nowhere does the circle close]. Indeed the circle never closes. Comparable is this ambiguity to the silence of fish. He wonders at the end where might be found the place of communication with the fish—or the ability, one might add, of recognizing anywhere the speaking of the fish in the nonspoken manner of the communication. This little sonnet tells us more about the poet's need for nonsemantic communication than anything since Rimbaud's cry, "trouver une langue."

But the negative expressions suggesting noncommunication or ineffable communication had been exhausted by the Symbolist *cénacle*. It was through simulated transgression into other arts that the postsymbolists were to identify the notion of unspeakable language, principally through imitation of music and dance. As we have mentioned earlier, Valéry had already suggested that after Mallarmé it was hard to speak of the powers of the dance, and its implications for poetry. Yet, through his reading of Valéry more than of Mallarmé, Rilke was also impressed by the mythopoetic transfer of dance into poetry. He was indeed to go further than his two predecessors and incorporate it within a larger context, which I would call calisthenics, or expression through movement. Dancer, acrobat, clown, and rider are all crystallizations of movement, all aspiring to the ultimate "Figur," and all so far removed from Rilke's original perspective, inspired by Rodin, of the static beauty of art in stone.

The basic fact is that calisthenics as an art is perhaps farthest removed from correspondences, or interpretations of nature, and therefore the closest to a realization of the fiction of the artist. The dancer does not interpret but transforms. He or she transforms ordinary movement to such an extent that its connection with natural phenomena is as remote as the distinction Apollinaire perceived between objects existing in nature and man's created products, such as the wheel. The movements of the dancer are studied and artificial, and minimally imitative of natural, spontaneous gestures. Nor is there a true mediator or interpreter, since the performer is at the same time the object of the performance. The human being does not create the art in this instance, but becomes the art. And the dichotomy between the creator and the created is nonexistent because the purpose of the art is in fact to establish a unity between the maker and what is made. Mallarmé, in his moments of utter disenchantment with the ephemeral character of the human condition, would sever the bonds of the artist with his work of art so that the work of art would have a chance to attain its own immortality.

In the case of Rilke's dancer who becomes the dance, that division is no longer conceivable. Nowhere has Rilke expressed this union so well without recourse to philosophical language but through a purely poetic image as in "Tanzt die Orange" (Part 1, Sonnet 15). Here, after suggesting a number of colors, flavors, countenances, tastes, and textures, all pertinent to a subject to be interpreted in standard fashion, he suddenly reveals the glorious difference: "Sie hat sich kostlich zu euch bekehrt" [It has been marvelously turned into you]. The metamorphoses of the dancer have produced the inexpressible condensation of meaning that a standard metaphor could never convey. The single word "orange" is capitalized as a universal substantive to which are opened the doors of interpretation—like a tone row in serial music composition, or like the haunting first line of Mallarmé's "Le vierge, le vivace et le bel aujourd'hui." The color or glow or shape of the orange becomes more hermetic in its total explicitness than even the negation of explicitness with which Mallarmé defined his notion of the pure object in terms of the flower absent from all bouquets. Here the common orange, present in all baskets of fruit, invites relationships: "Verwandtschaft," melding of rind and juice, that is, of the tangible and the flowing, of memory and immanence, of the capturable and the uncaptured.

In Part 2, Sonnet 18, the definition of dance is expressed through the common etymological meaning of the word "Vergehen" in opposition with "Gang"—the dancer is a translator of the passing uncaptured movement into a totally delineated act. In Sonnet 28 he is indeed the "Tanzfigur," an Orpheus-poet figure that has excelled nature: "darin wir die dumpf ordnende Natur / vergänglich übertreffen" [There we surpass in short order that order-giving Nature].

The most famous dance figure is, of course, that of Vera, who, in terms of her known biographical data, is dying. If from the human point of view the poem is the most touching one, like all writing dealing with beauty and youth in the throes of death, from the point of view of poetic communication it is particularly noteworthy because it demonstrates how the metaphor of what is integral to the dance ceases when death is imminent, even as life ceases. She stops being the dancer—"Tänzerin erst"—and turns into bronze; that is, she loses the motion, which was the expression of her dance, which was equated with the expression of the poet's art as well. The sudden vision of the "open gate" through which she is to pass has none of the glory it would have had in a religious approach to death. Instead it is "trostlos," dreary—which as a word does not explain the negation of the suffix "-los," its openness having no attraction and no meaning. And the poetic communication stops short, its own openness suddenly shut down before the openness of death. The philosophical statement inherent but not expressed is that poetry is the expression of the living and not of the dead.

In these dance poems the fact that there is often no distinction between the dance and the dancer suggests the indivisibility of the poem from the poet. In Part 1, Sonnet 11, the poem about the rider in the sky, there is a double constellation, which Rilke's interpreters have tried to identify with an astronomical

87

connotation. Such meaning would stress the dichotomy. But for Rilke the two make one, and to confound the interpreter even more, as they ride, the rider and the horse become the road, the target toward which they are riding. The sense of *drive* they communicate is the very nature of existence. Again what Rilke is doing is to suggest the indescribable motion of life, which he admits to be "namenlos," nameless, through a "Figur" fallen between heaven and earth in that indescribable space of "in-betweens." "Weg und Wendung" consists of the use of two words together, which amalgamates the straight line and the bent, a sense of the anomaly of human nature perhaps; it is left to the readers to instill their own meaning of what human purpose and its deviations might be, and again Rilke manages to leave philosophical conclusion understood but not asserted. Here again, as in "Vergehen und Gang," we have phonemic assimilation or tropism between "Weg" and "Wend-ung" in challenge to their semantic opposition. The image of movement becomes part of the pattern, aiming at the formation of a constellation. It is a measurable paradigm, a metaphor of the concept of the artist who here becomes a rider, in unseiz-able movement, heading for amalgamation in his own constel-lation, the work of art. This poem contains the same analogies that exist in Yeats's image of the falconer in "The Second Coming"

We might recall that in the earlier Fifth Elegy there is the same basic analogy created around the metaphoric use of the character of the acrobat. But there the style is still very descrip-tive. The focus on the acrobat, presumably inspired by a Pi-casso painting, weakens the power of the analogy as the charac-ter of the acrobat is directly communicated and upstaged. The movements enter so clearly into recognizable contexts that in-deed they allow the character to be associated with something outside the poem. However, in the last part of the poem, where in more typical symbolist fashion Rilke communicates in nega-tions, he attempts to transpose a life situation into a nonlife and therefore noninterpretable context:

Und plotzlich in diesem muhsamen Nirgends, plotzlich
die unsägliche Stelle, wo sich das reine Zuwenig
unbegreiflich verwandelt—, um springt
in jenes leere Zuviel.
Wo die vielstellige Rechnung
zahlenlos aufgeht

[And suddenly in this belabored nowhere, suddenly / the unspeakable place where the pure Too-little / is inconceivably transformed, changes /into that vacant Too-much / where the compli-
cated calculation / is left unaccounted.]

"Nirgends," "unsägliche Stelle," "unergreiflich verwandelt,"
"in jenes leere Zuviel / Wo die vielstellige Rechnung / zahlenlos
aufgeht"—all these negative expressions constitute together a
positive situation. And in the very last section, characteristically he addresses himself to the Angel, the creature of the in-
between world, as he speculates about the place of which we
know nothing, a space we can reach only with our indescribable carpet. The carpet we must not forget, upon which the ac-
robats were dancing, is now moved to a raised level; the carpet
is another object created through the power to substitute the
symbol of one art for another, which was so significant in the
art of Mallarmé—as it also becomes important in Rilke's. Carpet is easel in poetry, the art of the in-between worlds, in the
quasi-divine world where the artist ventures.

Indeed the universe of Rilke is situated between the symbols
of the ephemeral and of the artificial, between what Mallarmé
called "la faute idéale de roses" and Yeats's golden bird that survives the rose failure. There are in Rilke's *Elegies* and *Sonnets* a
whole range of figures struggling between the condition of the
rose and that of the golden bird, metaphorically speaking, between expression of the poet's mortality and assertion of the
work's immortality, the two forces brought into poignant confrontation in Mallarmé's memorial poem to Edgar Allan Poe,
"Tel qu'en Lui-même enfin l'éternité le change."

If the image of *rose* represents human vulnerability, then the

sense of blossoming is the broader sense of the human condition, as opposed to the sense of the power of the artist to transcend the human. Rilke's struggle against the fragility of flowering is nowhere so strikingly evident as in his Sixth Elegy,
about the fig tree. The blooming of a tree is likened to the waiting period, deemed precarious, unproductive, ephemeral. It is
therefore no surprise, although original in choice, that Rilke
should choose the fig tree, which of all trees is the one that goes
directly to fruit and bypasses the blossom. So be it with the
creative poet denying the flower/life state to reach the fruit
state. The message of this poem has been taken by most of
Rilke's interpreters on face value; that is, the hero designated in
the poem is presumed to represent a warrior-hero without hint
of substitute analogies. On that level, the young warrior passes
to fruition as rapidly as the fig tree, without being given time
for blossoming. It would signify the state of those who die an
early death in glory; such a message would indeed make it a
truly elegiac poem. But in the contexts of symbolism and of the
reflections of the symbolist *écriture* in Rilke's poetry and in the
thematic of the rose concepts, I see the fig poem, with its analogy to the seed in the womb aspiring to become man, a deeper
analogy.

Going back to the assumption that, like many other symbolists, Rilke designates the poet/artist in names other than the ordinary garden variety, warrior and fig tree are also substitutions. Just as elsewhere the dancer, the musician, the rider, the
acrobat are manifestations and Figures of the poet, so here the
so-called Hero is again the poet who renounces the blossoming—that is, living the ordinary life—and surges forward to the
hazards of producing the immediate fruit. The analogy is further strengthened by the double-tiered meaning of the function
of the womb, that space among the spaces that Rilke seeks out,
of infinite ambiguities and potential, where as the allusion to
Jupiter and the swan legend ("wie der Gott in den Schwan")
confirms that the seed, among an infinite number of other
seeds, creates a fertility. As in the case of the myth of Jupiter

and Leda, the artist does not leave birth/creation to the chance character of human insemination; for his creation, always endowed with overtones of association with the divine, is not arbitrary but willed and straight on target. The analogy in praise of fruit/creation is not carried to closure, fortunately; for if it were, the poem would have become an overt allegory. But the implications, presented on the level of the natural selection of the hero figure, conjure the selection among the many, of the poet figure who bypasses ordinary living to reach not death but the fruit of his own creation, that is, the work of art. In this context the abbreviated, terse line "Sein Aufgang ist Dasein" [His departure is a becoming] collates renouncement and becoming, which is perhaps one of the most apt definitions of poet from among the long series attempted by poets of the late nineteenth and early twentieth centuries to detour the common signifier "poet" from its usual signification. This is in strict opposition to the "Wir," that is, what the rest of us do, also expressed in terse terms: "Wir aber verweilen / ach, uns rühmt erst zu blühn" [But we remain, alas, we relish the blossoming]. He puts in sharp contrast the lot of the rest of us with the lot of the true poet, juxtaposing the poverty of our blooming with the glory of his privation of the rose condition in favor of the more rapid possession of the fruit.

If in the Sixth Elegy Rilke makes the image of the fig tree a source of innumerable conjectures as to how one may express indirectly the sense of being a poet, in others he offers another object: the tricky treatment of the mirror image. The mirror is a common symbolist image, much used and abused in coterie symbolist poetry. It has been accepted of course as the locus of narcissism, the contemplation of the self as the Other. Its dialogism has consisted traditionally in serving as a parallel to the reflection of the natural. Functionally the mirror is not a space for ambiguity. But as previously noted, Valéry changed that concept, giving the mirror a value-added quality, a more perfect image of the self leading to the very annihilation of the original self.

We see Rilke transform the mirror image in his own fashion, particularly in the Second and Third Sonnets of Part 2, where he questions the accepted connotations of mirror function and answers them. Using the same substitution device as Mallarmé, in his poet denotation here he appropriates the more general term of "Master," catching the sure stroke on the random "white page," here described as "das eilig / nähere Blatt" [the closest sheet on hand], and in an unusual handling of the metaphor structure, he makes the consequential part precede what should normally have been the onset of the metaphor, the concretely discernible object. But adding to the novelty, that tangible, presumably comprehensible part, that of "Spiegel," transgresses its ordinary connotation and enters directly into the ambiguous sphere of the Master's stroke on paper. He turns the mirror function into as ambiguous an activity as the master/ paper relationship of the first part of the analogy; for it is a selective mirror that he is talking about, one that retains only a choice image—the example given is that of the freshness of a maiden's smile. But it could be so many other faces and glances once we are prepared to relate the selection to the fortuitous capture on the part of the poet of the empty, random page of the first two lines! As the poet invades the space of the page/ mirror he endeavors to name the unnamed illuminations of the Earth, and actually becomes aware of lost visions making of the mirror/page a symbol of creative frustration.[5]

Rilke is close to Mallarmé's struggle with the frustration of the empty page, and if Mallarmé represented that struggle in the white plume of the swan caught in the ice of a lake, and plume/feather/pen in lake/mirror, catalyzed the image of potentially innumerable flights unflown, then Rilke projects the impossible in terms of an image of a heart singing in recognition

[5] It is interesting to observe that a little later on, under the aegis of surrealism, Paul Eluard would go a step further and make the mirror—this time without silvering—an instrument not to capture visions but to suggest the power *to give sight* ("donner à voir"). A few years and a whole poiesis separate Rilke from Eluard.

of its "Ganze geborne" in its literal translation "born into the Whole"—ambiguous although positive in statement, for the affirmative semantic structure negates the credibility of its signification. In the presentation of the ideal poet born with the knowledge of the total unity of experience, he opens the way for all the objections one will immediately raise to the possibility of such a birth, just as we reject the mirror function of selective retention proposed by the poet since we know that the signified meaning of mirror is to reflect only the passing reality. Rilke destroys the accepted meaning of mirror by making the image of the mirror the tool of the deconstruction of its meaning. Art is indeed the "Doppelbereich" for Rilke, a mirror that, instead of being a duplicate existence, becomes an object in which time and space are melded in "Zwischenraüme der Zeit" [the in-between space of time], where the poet, instead of being a reflector of life, practices the gamut of transformation: "wird ein Starkes über dieser Nahrung / Geh in der Verwandlung aus und ein" [Will gain strength from the nourishment /Go back and forth through transformation] (Sonnet 29, the last of Part 2).

To return to the sequence of the Second and Third Sonnets, Rilke proceeds from Master in no. 2 to Narcissus in no. 3. But of course the interpreter, now wary of common denotations or their extended connotations, will have to quickly discard the accepted archetype, as was the case in Valéry's treatment of the Narcissus theme. The original myth would have us believe that the beautiful youth sees his reflection and does not recognize it; then, in the first revision of the myth, Narcissus does recognize himself and loiters at the water's edge to enjoy his own beauty. As we have seen, Valéry's departures from the accepted solipsistic meaning of Narcissus created countermeanings in defiance of both mythology and semantics by his attraction to something that was not visible because it was the projection of an *interior* state. If we need the mirror to know how our exterior looks, how much more powerful must be the agent that may reveal our depth of being. The endeavor takes us to the outer junction of life and death. Valéry's objective was the expression of his poetic curiosity as to the quality of that site. Rilke's treatment of the Narcissus is more terse but perhaps more subtle, less reliant on cerebral self-control. He begins in no. 3 with a typically Germanic philosophical question about the true nature of the mirror object and its meaning: "Spiegel: noch nie hat man wissend beschrieben, / was ihr in eurem Wesen seid" [Mirror: never has anyone yet knowingly described what you really are].

But in the very word "wissend" preceded by "noch nie," that is, "not yet," he is challenging human knowledge and wisdom in the apprehension of the mirror meaning, in its true essence, and the subjunctive of the verb "to be," "seid," at the end of the second line, although grammatically inevitable, triggers in the reader the thought that Rilke is suggesting a dubious attitude as to the possibility of ever finding out. All this would seem to be presenting the obvious in ambiguous terms if we did not know that the mirror as well as the Narcissus is a fictitious use of the signifier in relation to the accepted signified reality. We will never know the true meaning of "mirror" because the poet has grave doubts about the special meaning he is giving it. Its site, typical of the unusual sites explored by Rilke, lies somewhere between space and time! Was there ever a better definition of the function of *poet* than that of a being in search of that ambiguous space between the temporal and the spatial, partaking of both but falling in the interval of two unequatable parts of an impossible equation. If then we can assume the mirror to be the fictitious space of the poet's reality, it takes a luster of the highest brilliance, sixteen-light candelabra to penetrate the space that is impenetrable; again the sense of the forbidding space is achieved through the association of a very concrete object in the exterior world with a vision dependent solely on the possibilities in the German language to create compatibilities of signification previously nonexistent: "Und der Lüster geht wie ein Sechzehn-Ender / durch eure Unbetretbarkeit" [And the luster goes like a sixteen-pointer through your impenetrability].

In the next two tercets the mirror identifying with the poetic process focuses on the selective power of poetic choice, which discards many a painting or poem to release to permanent viewing only the most beautiful. Resistant to paraphrase are the last two lines, and thereby they become the most powerful: Rilke envisions the encounter of the selective mirror with Narcissus/poet at the junction where Narcissus seems to plunge toward some unseen but glorious prize in a journey that in its ambiguity becomes reminiscent of the last stanza of Baudelaire's "Le Voyage."

> Aber die Schönste wird bleiben, bis
> drüben in ihre enthaltenen Wangen
> eindrang der klare gelöste Narziss.

[But the most beauteous will remain until / on her forbidden cheeks / the bright freed Narcissus put his imprint.]

Without being long-winded like Valéry, Rilke achieves that same sense of poetic *ascesis* and ontological peril in Narcissus's search rather than the recognition of beauty.

The Fourth Sonnet, about the unicorn, is as total a model of poetic fiction as Mallarmé's Faun, Valéry's *La Jeune Parque*, and Yeats's golden bird of Byzantium. The unicorn is nurtured by lovers (creative process), exists in space created by them, is *pure* in the sense of being stripped of normal attributes, and is simultaneously incorporated within a virgin (the unconceived; by extension, the unwritten) and into the mirror (the selective memory box); the double entry is the same kind of amalgamation of experience and creative construction as the leitmotif that emerges in Mallarmé's account of that unforgettable afternoon of the Faun following the morning of the orgy-dream. Like Mallarmé, and like Valéry, Rilke has chosen a standard mythological figure as the point of departure for his deconstruction-reconstruction process. The unicorn, a fabulous bird clearly identifiable in known mythology and therefore a collective point of reference, becomes the target of the poet's protest against its too-clearly defined position as an accepted reality of

95

the mythological space. The poem sets out to refashion mythology by his fresh source of creative artifice. For Rilke the most important power of the animal is its "Wandeln" power of *change*, just as the unseizable phases of change in the dancer fascinated him. This quality, more than any other, emphasizes potentiality: "Zwar war es nicht" [It never really was].

The poet must be emphatic, almost redundant, to illuminate the unreality of the animal that owes its life purely to poetic creativity: fed on love/creativity and not on corn, it lives on possibility, "Möglichkeit," in a space created by the lovers/poets—and out of this nothing that is everything, he was nurtured to grow a horn. Its artifice despoiled, it can only renew itself by plunging again into fiction, "Silber-Spiel," and fresh reality, "Zu seiner Jungfrau," to refurbish its art:

> Sie nahren es mit keinem Korn,
> nur immer mit der Möglichkeit, es sei,
> Und sie gab solche Stärke an das Tier,
> dass es aus sich ein Stirnhorn trieb. Ein Horn.
> Zu einer Jungfrau kam es weiss herbei—
> und war im Silber-Spiegel und in ihr.

[They did not feed it with any grain / yet ever with the possibility that it might be / And so gave the animal such strength / that it grew a horn on its brow. One horn. / To a maiden it came all in white / and resided in the silver-mirror and within her.]

We can read Sonnet 10 virtually as an *ars poetica* if we follow the substitution process of the poem, pitting the arts against the machine. In the struggle with the utilitarian life, art is to take the initiative away from "Leben" to which it opposes "Dasein," the progressive wonderment created by the poet. Its source is primordial, as suggested by the use of the word "Ursprung" [root], which has both a physical and a philosophical sense. Followed by "Ein Spielen von reinen / Kräften" [A game of pure skills], it brings about an intertwining of fame and power for magic, suggesting once more the notion of poet as hero/force. The adjective "rein" intervenes not as a moral meaning but in the undiluted sense in which Mallarmé used "pure" and Rilke attributed the notion to the Jungfrau in the earlier sonnet, on the same register as Mallarmé's "le vierge, le vivace et le bel aujourd'hui." The power of becoming a source of wonder in "a hundred places" refers, as we know, to those unlocated places. The final contrast between machine and song/art/poetry releases the absent quality of "Unsäglichen" relating to language; in the last instance Rilke cannot avoid an overt transfer from music to language, to confront the corporeal presence of machine, which begrudgingly makes room for music/language and its sacred character in the spaces that are unusable in the perspective of the materialistic value-scale of the world in opposition to the values of the artist. It is in these useless spaces that art will build its divine temple: house built with stone, but stone out of which music gushes. Although it is hard to prove—and were it easy it would not be worth the speculation—the "bebendsten Steinen" also partake of the making of art. Thus the substitutions would be more total if seen to combine the work in stone with the work on paper, and the work of music.

The search for the inexpressible leads Rilke to the recognition of the "Figur" as a creature of turning, of transformation ("Verwandlung"); but although many poets before and after him have been fascinated by metamorphosis, in the case of Rilke's vision *it is the power to transform rather than the state gained by the transformation that is most meaningful*. Through this distinction he achieves a subtler definition of the poet than a mere builder of phantasmagoria. The poet is not simply a being who overcomes the stasis by changing the stolid and the stale, but one who is able to perceive that imperceptible point/moment of the changing through participation in the process. He attempts to fix the point of transition, to capture the transient as it settles into eternal pose—casting the dancer's fleeting movement into the immobility of art, for example, as in Sonnet 28:

O komm und geh. Du, fast noch Kind, ergänze
für einen Augenblick die Tanzfigur
zum reinen Sternbild eines jener Tänze,

[Oh come and go. You, a mere child still, in the / blinking of an
eye the dance figure / with the pure constellation of one of those
dances.]

Obviously, the poem that crystallized transformation is Sonnet 13, about Daphne. If the Daphne of mythology is indeed the typical symbol of transformation, her function in this sonnet is altered in the manner in which other mythological figures are revised. She is not a being transformed but one who gives the power of transformation to the poet. The laurel that Daphne feels she has become is a static image, which can be identified with the image of glory only if she can move the poet to change into wind, that is, one who can shake and set into movement the old meanings, turn beginnings into ends and ends into beginnings.

The motive force of poetry is further subjected to metaphoric form in no. 13 in the unconventional use of the Eurydice figure: "Sei immer tot in Eurydike" [Be forever dead in Eurydice]. Here the mythological figure epitomizes the dead past to be overcome in the drive toward the unspeakable totality of meanings beyond the fixed ones of the past. The experience is fraught with pain as suggested in that powerful image of the glass that shatters in its ringing process: "sei ein klingendes Glas, dass sich im Klang schon zerschlug" [be a ringing glass that is shattered as it rings]. This image can be interpreted in many ways. If taken from the point of view of the craft of symbolist substitution, the glass that destroys itself in its own intensity may again suggest the condition of being a poet, a life-threatening condition that may lead to oblivion—"Nicht-Seins Bedingung" [the state of nonbeing]. Rilke finds himself on the same risky journey into nothingness as Mallarmé in his longer life span from *Igitur* to *Un Coup de dés*.

But a last-minute turning point away from the old pattern of the symbolist nihilism can be noted in the last two sonnets. Where Mallarmé questioned the viability of the poetic Word, Rilke gives images of triumph over "dumb nature." If nature forgets the poet, the power of speech takes control, appropriating nature's own functions, such as "ich rinne" and "Ich bin," with which the series ends. His assertive stance echoes Valéry's "Le vent se lève, il faut tenter de vivre" [The wind is rising, we must attempt to live], which was his final response to thoughts of dirge and mortality in *Le Cimetière marin*.

Rilke then participates in the pattern of a number of postsymbolist poets who, emerging from the fin-de-siècle nihilism, begin to overcome that state not by denying human vulnerability but rather through their confidence in the power of survival inherent in the poetic idiom. They had found through the Symbolists before them the linguistic devices that might make possible the survival of the signifier to the things it signified in a given period, a form of semantic transcendence more rationally acceptable to the era than earlier metaphysical assumptions of supernal existence.

If that sense of possible escape from the human condition is indicated in poems about death by Mallarmé, particularly as previously mentioned in some of his "Tombeau" pieces, his aspirations are often congealed in the sole "hope of the corridor." "Perhaps" is a whimper often repeated but with small conviction in *Un Coup de dés*. The miracle of artistic survival was the only hope for a whole generation oppressed by the reduction of the signifier "ciel" to a purely physical signification. The removal of the concept and image of "heaven" from the universe of the poet was a rupture whose magnitude is hard to realize for post-apocalyptic generations. It shifted a much-needed anchorage to language, making it more than an instrument of interpretation or mediation. For when belief in one of the poles is diminished, or indeed if it is obliterated, language can no longer serve as an intermediary. It becomes a pole itself, delimiting the space between mouth of Earth or Man and preserver of the poetic cognizance. The ontological direction of poetry is from priest to god, from temple sheltering the scripture to "Haus" generating a new scripture. Poetic language turns from deciphering to a force for becoming: "Dasein" leads to "Wandlung." The forest of symbols has become an open space outside the interpreted world; Rilke deplored in the Sixth Elegy through the mouth of the Angel that the space was being neglected, but in the Daphne sonnet it has become a happy, even lucky space, "glückliche Raum," where the transformation can occur. The triumphant last sonnet achieves discovery of the spot where the crossing of the senses creates the defiant, ultimate sense/spirit of space possessed.

In this interspace between the mortal and immortal, between earth and sky, the poet is Orpheus, Angel, Daphne, Narcissus, and that compelling force in the undeterminable guise of "Figur," inhabiting, as Rilke best described it in the Fifth Elegy, a lower sky: "Vorstadt-Himmel der Erde."

The Mallarméan artifacts survive and are revised: the rose without a name that is pure "glow" overcoming the rose condition, the unicorn whose horn is the fiction added to the state of pure animal, the dancer who becomes the spirit of dance and whose movement is finally fixed in bronze, the mirror that is a container instead of a reflector, and Narcissus who searches for something other than himself.

Interpreters of Rilke's poetry attribute to him loftier thoughts than those encapsulated in these images. In fact, reference is made more often to the overtly expressed philosophical statements in those texts where he addresses the reader more directly than in the poems cited here. But his contribution to modern poetics is more valid in the unasserted spaces of his poetic writings. He is most meaningful in terms of the symbolist reading of his work when he is least voluble and less defined in meaning; in this sense the *Sonnets* are the most illustrative of a reading that puts him in the lineage of Mallarmé rather than in that of the philosophically inclined German Romanticists. Whereas the use of the legitimate spaces for human poetry are often entrenched in theological dichotomies, the *Sonnets* assume the new direction; they are more difficult to read unilaterally but are more universally readable. The old symbols turn to new, transformed significations. Orpheus defies his mythological destiny by taking control of what was to be his destruction. In becoming the mouth of Nature and the top branch of the Tree he has a chance to speak of the unspeakable. His regeneration is the symbol of the re-creation of the Earth according to art. In forgetting the given names of things he opens the path to renaming them:

> Erde, ist es nicht dies, was du willst: unsichbar
> in uns erstehen?—Ist es dein Traum nicht,
> einmal unsichbar zu sein?

[Earth, is this not what you want: to stand unseen within us?— Is this not your dream / To be sometime invisible?] (Ninth Elegy)

Rilke accomplished the principal functions that Mallarmé had assigned to the poet—he questioned the nature of the mirror, that is, mimesis, and defied the fragility of the Orpheus destiny in surviving the rose condition:

> Ein für alle Male
> ist Orpheus, wenn er singt. Er kommt und geht
> Ists nicht schon viel, wenn er die Rosenschale
> um ein paar Tage manchmal übersteht?"

[Once and for all / it is Orpheus if there is singing. He comes and goes. / Is it not sufficient that he survives by a few days the bowl of roses?] (Part 1, Sonnet 5)

The dream of Mallarmé to suggest and not to describe found in Rilke the poetic site, the undescribable space where the transitory quality of man is transformed into the most enduring expression of his art. Confusing the poem with the poet, commentators have been in the habit of calling the *Sonnets* the song of a dying swan. In the perspective of the symbolist tradition, the present tense of the verb in "ich bin," which ends the *Sonnets*, has the same powerful defiance of fleeting time and evanescence as the ending of *The Afternoon of a Faun*, the transient signified in terms that make it permanent.

Yeats and the Symbolist Connection

Iɴ ᴠɪᴇᴡ of the extensive critical writings on Yeats by Richard Ellmann, Denis Donoghue, Helen Vendler, and Harold Bloom, to mention only a few of the better known, it becomes presumptuous to have to add anything but passing remarks such as those I have already made in my book on the Symbolist Movement. Moreover, in the face of the heavily documented national heritage with which Yeats's work has become identified, it becomes virtually a work of diplomacy to extricate it for other levels of consideration. Yet Yeats indubitably holds a definite position in the international context of those of his fellow poets with whom he has developed the modern fiction of the poet. This fiction has tangential relations with known mythologies but is not identical to them. Heretofore Yeats's appropriations of the fantastic religious visions have been strictly associated in the critical view with Celtic legend and gnostic concepts. Departures from the binational context of his affiliations—English literature and Irish legend—have been extended only to considerations of philosophic influences from abroad; but a paraphrase or two of Nietzsche or a skirting of gnostic philosophers does not constitute poetry. It is surprising how little mention there is in the major works on Yeats about the symbolist factor and of the contact with Mallarmé, begrudgingly admitted although it goes far beyond conjecture in view of the overt references in the writings of Yeats as well as those merely reported by others.

Even as the Celtic heritage has been expounded, the foreign influences or impacts have been deemed "dubious" in the classic interpretations of Yeats. But his own awareness of his affiliations with Mallarmé and with the Symbolists and postsymbolists can be gleaned in his letters, his autobiography, his memoirs, and his essays. The allusions are stated in generalities. They make it evident that he had a sense of proximity with the Symbolist group, and that Arthur Symons and Ernest Dowson were his intermediaries in the comprehension of specific texts. His letters on poetry allude to Mallarmé and to Maeterlinck as well as to Swedenborg. But I hasten to add, as I have maintained in my general perceptions of Symbolism elsewhere, that the Swedenborgian philosophy and symbolization are more closely associable in all these poets with a lingering Romanticism than with the symbolist mode's ingrained philosophy. Swedenborgian symbolism is Christian and dualistic whereas those espousing the inspiration of the Symbolist movement are skirting a somewhat pagan form of mysticism.

Yeats's connection with Symbolism is made clear in his *Autobiographies*,[1] where he gives full credit to Symons for having brought him into contact with the Mallarmé group. Although Yeats had been in Paris and had even witnessed a performance of Villiers de l'Isle-Adam's *Axel* (which is an avatar of Romanticism rather than symbolist theater), Yeats's experience with symbolist poetry is largely through readings of Symons: "My thoughts gained . . . richness and clearness from his sympathy, nor shall I ever know how much I owe to the passages that he read me from Catullus and from Verlaine and Mallarmé" (*Autobiographies*, 192). Of his reading of *Axel* he says, "I could without much effort imagine that here at last was the Sacred Book I longed for" (192). And of Mallarmé in particular: "I think that those [readings] from Mallarmé may have given form to my verses of those years, to the later poems of *The Wind among the Reeds*, to *Shadowy Waters* . . . (193).

Elsewhere Yeats observes that when at his request someone went through his work to cross out "conventional metaphors,"

---

[1] Yeats, *Autobiographies* (London, 1927), including "The Trembling of the Veil," 192 and 193.

he was shocked to find that "they seem to have rejected also those dream associations which were the whole art of Mallarmé."[2] And when he praises Symons's *The Symbolist Movement* but regrets that he cannot praise it enough because it is dedicated to him, he emphasizes Symons's quote from Mallarmé that is at the heart of symbolist imagery by requoting it: "the horror of the forest or the silent thunder in the leaves."

But such exterior evidences would be of no consequence if there were not significant scriptural resonances to establish the serial proximities with the major cluster of poets under scrutiny.

In dealing with the symbolist aspects of Yeats's work here, as in the other chapters, I will be selective with an eye only for those pieces that show the symbolist technique of terse and open-ended communication that defies analytic attempts at exterior deciphering or decoding of ambiguities of meaning. For the focus is Yeats's particular contribution to the *meaning of meaning* in poetry, what he himself viewed in "The Symbolism of Poetry" as "the subtleties that have a new meaning every day," and which is indeed the far-reaching contribution of the symbolist mode to the general field of poetics and, by extension, to that of linguistics as well.

Yeats entered the symbolist forum in two separate ways. One, strikingly demonstrable in *Shadowy Waters* and *Deirdre*, sharing the mystique of Maurice Maeterlinck, was a conceptual and spiritual affinity that he expressed in his two major essays on Symbolism as the poet's reaction to the empirical world of technological progress. He viewed the problematics of his response, as Mallarmé had done before him, in terms of the need for a secular priesthood. Indeed, Yeats turned the creation of art into a sacred function. We read in "The Celtic Element in Literature": "The arts in brooding upon their own intensity have become religious and are seeking . . . to create a sacred book." Again, in "The Autumn of the Body," he writes, "The

[2] In *A General Introduction to My Work* (New York, 1968).

105

arts are, I believe, about to take upon their shoulders the burdens that have fallen from the shoulders of priests."

But the second association of Yeats with symbolism is closer to the postsymbolist poetics and its implicit mystique observed in the current study. It has to do with the symbolist *écriture*. A close reading of a famous sentence in his article "The Symbolism of Poetry" shows the distinction. Yeats says, "How can the arts overcome the slow dying of men's hearts that we call the progress of the world, and lay their hands upon men's heartstrings again, without becoming the garment of religion as in old times?" "Garment" implies something exterior; its rejection shows Yeats's awareness that writing has to have a self-contained transfer of human experience into artistic manifestation independently of theological persuasions. Unlike Mallarmé, Yeats never abandons the possibility of spiritual transcendence, nor does he express any overt intention to make language do something it has not done before; but he does achieve in some of his poems that transformation of the language of communication into a language which creates its own vision through a morphological lens that distorts the exterior dimensions of reality.

From this perspective two different faces of Yeats emerge. One is familiar. It contains the features of a poet alienated from worldly concerns but who is, as his staunchest admirers convincingly demonstrate, eventually cured of that malady and learns to face the real world after he has yearned for the inexpressible and talked about mystery. The other consists of the assiduous alchemist in those instances less frequent but more pertinent to this reading, where he creates *in language* the mystery and the artificial world where things, through poems, escape the mortality of the creator.

I have in my previous work[3] discussed "Leda and the Swan" as one such model of the postsymbolist poem; there are others

---

[3] Anna Balakian, *The Symbolist Movement: A Critical Appraisal* (New York, 1967; reprint, New York, 1977).

that deserve critical attention and fall into this serial continuity of symbolist *écriture*. But before dealing with individual poems, the basic avenue on which these poetic patterns were to be structured might be recalled.

The primary one was Yeats's struggle with history. So entrenched in his mind was this negative attitude toward history that the highest compliment he could pay Mallarmé was, as mentioned earlier, to commend him for having escaped history. The nineteenth century was the age of history; it acknowledged history as a pseudoscience, it gave events historical evaluation, and in vying with historical writing, literary authors aimed to give their works historical context. This trend gave narrative structure a larger importance than most poets were willing to concede to it. Richard Wagner was one of the first to protest against history and to suggest the substitution of legend as a framework for the arts in its power to intensify narrative sequence and to allow the artist to give the passage of time a more subjective comprehension. But for the most sophisticated of the Symbolists the use of the legend as an alternative to historical narration could not be a candid appropriation of the known content of legend. That would simply permit the intrusion of the element of the fantastic into the truth factor of history and support the usual treatment of the dichotomy between legendary and empirical reality. The prevalent notion that created a mere antithesis between the legendary and the historical was too facile, too antithetical. Negative interpretations of the historical would be too close to the previous Romantic notions of the fantastic or the uncanny, or even of the sacred. These poets aimed to go beyond the dualistic interpretations of existence espoused by the apostles of Swedenborg. The structures of legend rather than its known subject matter was what interested them and what they would include in their poetic strategies.

Yeats, viewing legend as an alternative to history, incorporated into the matrix of many of his poems the element of circularity intrinsic to the process whereby legend functions as a distinct dimension in his poems. It is manifest in his image of the gyre, in the phases of the moon, in his rotation of comings and goings of the swans at Coole, and in the returns of ominous visions. But if his appropriations of legendary materials were limited to this particular practice, he would be "symbolist" only in his way of thinking of event and not necessarily in his *écriture*. The Irish legends he utilizes would have been only a substitution for the overworked classical or Biblical ones more currently used. In fact he did think in those terms as early as 1897 when he wrote, "The Irish legends move among known woods and seas, and have so much of a new beauty that they may well give the opening century its most memorable symbols" ("The Symbolism of Poetry").

Yeats was to alter the Celtic materials as the classical settings were modified by Mallarmé and Valéry, and the changes that occur in the identification of the Celtic myth were as normal for Yeats as those wrought in Mallarmé's eclogue of the Faun or in the perception of La Jeune Parque and of Narcissus in the work of Valéry. The evocation of the myth for Yeats, as for the others, is a distancing process, an effort to place the voice of the poet in a temporal vacuum. So great is Yeats's desire to free himself from time that he links in the same vision Celtic characters separated by centuries from each other and on a different time scale from him. In his own notes to "The Wanderings of Oisin" he observes, "The events it describes, like the events in most of the poems of this volume, are supposed to take place in the indefinite period made up of many periods, described by the folk tales, than in any particular century."[4]

It is ironic that in so many studies on Yeats the historical linkage of his myths is stressed whereas he actually utilizes myths to evade history because of its unavoidable association with measured time. Instead, Yeats stresses through these characters that bear the mark of artifice a reflection of himself in their phantasmagoric transparency even as the waters reflect

[4] *Collected Poems of W. B. Yeats* (London, 1933).

108

the face of a changed Narcissus for Valéry. Such characters carry in their being youth and old age simultaneously as a resounding distinction from the human whom time can take only in a single direction toward aging and dying. Art finds its defense against mortality in the stance of the mythic figure that may actually have no resemblance, except in its name, to the traditional myth figure generally recognized.

Yeats's use of mythic figures actually helps transcend the dichotomy between life and death just as surely in the Celtic as we shall see it do in the Byzantine. For instance, in *Shadowy Waters*, it is futile to stress the conciliation of opposites in the characters of Dectora and Fraegel by suggesting that one is seeking life and the other death. Their conjunction results from a pact for them to clear out of the world that lives by those very terms. Their disappearance into the deep void of the sea is in truth a passage, a transposition from life to canvas; it marks their entry into the world of art where they have ceased to perform in the temporal world in order to become the immortal performance.

Thus did Yeats himself escape from history, as he perceived Mallarmé to have done before him. In Yeats's case the feat was much harder because in his own history-bound time span he was much more involved with historical events than Mallarmé had been in a similar period of turmoil. There is no doubt that a fuller temporal political life is as much reflected in Yeats's work as the artificial temporal stasis that can be observed in some of his poems. Yeats's range is broader than Mallarmé's; the poetry of immobility and the poetry of action were to cohabit in his art even as we shall see in the case of Wallace Stevens and Jorge Guillén. With all three poets, Mallarmé's way is only one of the many roads on which they ventured. According to Yeats's own comment in *The Trembling of the Veil*, "I must do all things that I may set myself into a life of action and express not the traditional poet but that forgotten thing, the normal man" (299). Never would Mallarmé have said such a thing, and in this assertion it is as if Yeats were fighting the Mallarmé alternative of the poet turning his back on life as it is normally lived.

Yeats assumed another feature of Mallarmé's alternatives to narration and description: the power to suggest effect, the sense of *degrees* of relationship between the inner and the outer worlds of the artist rather than the poles of that relationship. The elimination of historical truth weakens the empire of time upon thought and action. Focus on the levels of association rather than on the parts associated between mythical figures and the phantasms created by the poet would lift the burden of monotony that threatens the standard sequence of cause and effect. The interplay would be more subtle, and would lend itself to more numerous and contradictory interpretations, more resistent to definitive solutions. One of the tests of Yeats's achievements as a postsymbolist is precisely in those poems where his interpreters have difficulty finding points of agreement.

This ambiguity contributes most forcefully to the fiction of the poet in his ability to avoid the archetypical connotations assigned to legendary figures. In the cases of Mallarmé, Valéry, and Rilke, there are distortions of the meaning of the archetypes of the Faun, Hérodiade, Orpheus, and Narcissus. Of course, in choosing a whole new set of mythological figures Yeats deftly avoids an entire range of reinterpreted archetypes, and in adopting a series of legendary figures unfamiliar to his readers he is thereby less accountable to them. But even within that privileged context, the figures are chosen as personal emblems of his own poetic vision rather than for any psychological or even philosophical meanings that might be gleaned from the common sources of previous interpretations for the pleasure of Yeats's more knowledgeable readers. One has only to compare his Deirdre with more conventional ones. But in his case, more significant than the misinterpretations or reinterpretations of known legendary figures is the fact that Yeats participates in the creation of his own cast of legendary figures out of ordinary and real persons such as Michael Robartes without impelling readers to attribute any universal meaning for the legendary role. The effort is aimed strictly at creating an ambiguity for this figment of the imagination.

In proceeding now to some specific poems from the point of view of the symbolist optic, *The Vision*,[5] with its systematic and graphic conceptualization, will be totally avoided because it consists of emblems rather than symbols and is thereby conducive to systematic interpretations. If I mention it here it is to reaffirm that Yeats is only *partially* a symbolist, and his avoidance of total commitment is shared by all the other poets with whom I have associated him in this book. It is only by the addition, one with the other, of partial achievements in this direction that we can arrive at a unity in the creation of a poetics that in itself is too rigorous, too vertiginous to be exclusively practiced and sustained by any single poet.

In an early and rather direct dialogue, "Anashuya and Vijaya," calling on a legend few of his readers will recognize, Yeats characterizes Beauty in allegorical visualization as "pacing on the verge of things." The phrase is indicative of one of the stylistic devices whereby he extricates poetic reality from both the empirical and the subjective. This device was to be used frequently in later poems that will fall under our scrutiny. Here let us simply ask: what takes this phrase out of an antithetical dualistic mechanism? The words "verge" and "things" used in association with each other give to both a resonance that they would otherwise not have. "Verge" indicates ambiguity of position: in that context it is associable with all the symbolist poetry and drama of *waiting*. "Verge" also implies a turning point, and therefore the concentration on the bridge between states rather than on the juxtaposition of states. But there would have been limits on its power to generate ambiguity if it had been coupled with an abstract noun such as anger,

---

[5] See Helen Vendler's study of *The Vision* in *The Vision and the Later Plays* (Cambridge, Mass., 1963) and Harold Bloom's *Yeats* (New York, 1972). They do very close readings of the hieroglyphics and sources of its references.

fear, and so on, by offering the possibility of a decipherable equation. Instead, Yeats creates a poetic anomaly unleashed and allowed to gravitate toward concrete, graspable "things." By contaminating that core of material reality denoted by "things" the poet erases the known contours of figures in almost the same fashion as the solarized photographs of Man Ray, working in a later mode.

Also among the elements that can associate Yeats's work with the postsymbolist poets is his secularization of the intermediary angel as in Rimbaud, in Rilke, and, as we shall see, in Stevens. In the case of Yeats the angel takes the form of a Druid, but far from being identifiable with the acceptable image of the Druid in Celtic mythology it is his own special Druid, making out of this mythological reference not the usual quasi-divine interpreter of the supernal for man but the poet's own dialectical counterpart existing in an in-between world.

Yeats offers a nonhistorical world in which legendary figures are altered by the poet, and things as well as beings live in sites not compatible with reality yet not relegated to the beyond. Self-contained as a canvas, detached from the normal measurements of time—such is the world of artifice that emerges from many of Yeats's major poems.

The struggle against chronos, which is the linguistic effort to escape history, is already manifest, as indicated previously, in that early poem-drama, *Shadowy Waters*. The simplicity of its symbolist climate puts it in contrast to later poems that are more convincing vehicles to demonstrate a new semantics that attempts to obliterate old codes.

First of all, this play demonstrates what survives of Romanticism in the early Yeats. The word "magic" is used in terms of the Romantic perception as the words "strange" and "unheard"; also Romantic is the antithetical search for an existence freed of "the events of the world." The search for the pure woman to be forever loved, possibly through a suicide pact, is also a Romantic notion continued and resonating in Villiers's *Axel*, rather than a Symbolist theme.

112

But in spite of these prevailing Romantic tendencies, there are three new elements, two of them dealing with nonsequential use of chronos:

> The movement of time is shaken in these seas
> and what one does
> One moment has no night upon the moment
> That follows

Here is something beyond the simple sense of "forever" or "everlasting" because it attacks sequence and continuity, cause and its inevitable consequences; what we witness is an altered register of time. Though fragmental and passing here, it will have a referential importance when it is more fully developed in later poems. The other taunting of accepted dimensions of time is the most hypnotic line of all about space related to time, "where no child's born but to outlive the moon," implying an eternity beyond that of the natural everlastingness suggested by the image of the moon. The human power to imagine surpassing nature's permanence will also reemerge in later poems. Its importance to Yeats is evident in the fact that it is echoed in this text and in others, and is not a lyrical passing fancy.

The third element that distances the piece from Romanticism has to do with the introduction of the Druid in this dialogue for the first time, and after its initial identification it was to play a predicate role in Yeats's language, reinforcing its known attributes to suggest the power of artists. "Druid-craft" and "Druid-spell" launch a terse code conveying the same type of superpower of language as "to outlive the moon." These expressions are used in the same manner as Mallarmé's "faute idéale de roses," in which, as we have seen, "Rose" is a seepage of the identifiable qualities of the flower normally designated as "la rose." Yeats puts the reader in a similar situation; he does not expect Druid to be used as a qualifier rather than as a noun with a stated meaning, even if its reference is mythological. We would expect "the craft of the Druid" or "the spell of the Druids"; instead the adjectival use of the name goes on in a series

113

that includes "Druid moons," "Druid apple-wood," and so forth. *Shadowy Waters* might have been a simple mood play were it not for the factor of substitutions of signifiers, so dominant in Mallarmé, that can be observed here changing the dreamlike, ephemeral vision into something static but substantial, enduring as a "thing" or artifact, as if cast on canvas. "The lasting watchers," having a demiurgic function, give Forgael his "old harp." But it is no more a harp than the Faun's flute was a flute in Mallarmé's poem. In both cases we have a substitution for the pen of the poet and its power to transcend both reality and the dream through the work of art.

The power of the artist to recuperate the "waste seas," reminiscent of T. S. Eliot's wasteland, into the art that blooms forever, is characterized as being "more mighty than sun and moon / Or the shimmering net of the stars." The image of the royal couple detached from time and moving into undetermined space contains the seeds of the later and more elaborate "Sailing to Byzantium." The Druid-power as well as the passage from natural ground to the lasting space of art was to become an element of reference throughout Yeats's poetry.

In the collection entitled *The Rose* it is interesting to note that the symbol of the Rose is not the mystically eternal one we are accustomed to in religion and medieval romance, but the concept tendered by Mallarmé of frailty and perishability reminiscent of the human condition that Yeats is trying to convey:

> Beauty grown sad with its eternity
> Made you of us, and of the dim grey sea

Although explicit, it forewarns us not to look for the Rose merely as an element of the supernal in the code language of Yeats. It is the Rose of the Symbolists, not of the Rosicrucians—although we cannot deny that the other is used elsewhere in more conventional context as "inviolate Rose."[6]

---

[6] Yeats's critics make a central issue of the Rosicrucian rose; see particularly Richard Ellmann's iconography in *The Identity of Yeats* (New York, 1954). Ellmann's interpretations assign specific meanings in terms of strictly Chris-

"The Hosting of the Sidhe" presents us with a double register of significations: if the Sidhe is a people of the Faery Hills, it is also an appellation of the wind, the whirling wind; and therefore in what ensues its use will offer two levels of meaning in uneven correspondences that include "the dance of the daughters of Herodias." Another interesting element in the early and rather conventional collection *The Wind among the Reeds* is the refrain in "The Withering of the Boughs":

> No boughs have withered because of the wintery wind;
> The boughs have withered because I have told them my dreams.

The important thing here is that the poet has begun to compete with nature rather than to be simply its interpreter. This perception suggests godlike powers even as it has been observed in Rilke and in others in the process of fashioning their own landscapes.

But so far these are small items. If Yeats's contact with Mallarmé dated from the 1890s the sustained symbolistic *écriture* does not emerge in his writings until 1919 and is particularly effective in the 1920s, precisely at the very moment that postsymbolist poetry is at its peak in other parts of the literary

---

tian symbols. He calls the continuous pursuit of rose references "the gamut of roses," and although he associates the Yeats roses with Dante, the Virgin Mary, and the poetry of Lionel Johnson and Ernest Dowson, it does not occur to him to refer to Mallarmé's quite different use of the rose image, nor does it occur to him that Yeats might have used the rose quality in more than one reference system. In fact it is extraordinary that in view of the meticulous search Ellmann did within English literature for connections between Yeats and his English and Celtic forebears and contemporaries, he did not think of looking for some importations from France to create a more universal mix. Ellmann is just one example of the many Yeats specialists who wear blinders where foreign affiliations are concerned. When Ellmann says that Yeats consumed Oscar Wilde's aesthetic system and talks of the "symbolic" rather than "symbolist" qualities of Yeats's plays, his thoroughness in Anglo-Saxon source search makes the omission of the French impact all the more glaring. An exception is Haskell Block, "Yeats, Symons, and the Symbolist Movement in Literature," in Richard J. Finneran, ed., *Yeats: An Annual of Critical and Textual Studies* 8 (1990): 9–18.

world, evidenced by a whole cluster of masterpieces that reached publication in the early part of the 1920s. They brought to an apogee, incongruently and after the fact, the expression of an era that had vanished with World War I.

The first poem of the series of *The Wild Swans at Coole* has been the subject of many commentaries, particularly on its biographical implications connected with the circumstances of Yeats's visit at Coole, which explains the real, human reasons for its melancholy tone. And indeed the first parts of the poem, if at all associable with symbolism, have an affinity with Verlaine's desolate park atmosphere of "Colloque sentimental":

> Autumn was over him; and now they stood
> On the lone border by the lake once more

echoes:

> Dans le vieux parc solitaire et glacé
> Deux spectres ont évoqué le passé.

The cyclic movement of the poem, which does not seem to defy any chronometrical system, is even quite specific in its numerical designation of nineteen years. It is only when we reach the last stanza that something unusual occurs in terms of its semantic structure:

> But now they drift on the still water
> Mysterious, beautiful

Why *now*? Why this sudden transpositional present? Why their sudden break with habit? Simply because the poet wills it so, in the same way as the boughs wither when he casts on them his dream. There is here a turn of signification whereby the poet detours the swans' historical pattern by the cessation of the dream; we are jolted because until he said "when I awake" we were not aware that he was giving us a dream sequence rather than one set in reality. Here we have an excellent example not of the juxtaposition or polarization of two states, the dream and the real, but the *effect* of the association; in the spirit of

116

Mallarmé, not the forest, not the thunder, but the effect of the thunder on the forest. Yeats conveys the same type of ambivalence as at the end of Mallarmé's *Afternoon of a Faun*, when we are not sure whether we, along with him, were dreaming or recalling. But we are sure, as in Mallarmé's poem, that the ambivalence is the effect of a poetic creation that amalgamates the dream with reality into his world of artifice where the Romantic fashion would have been to create an antithesis between the two states. The sudden cessation of cyclical movement is like the cessation of human movement, making an indirect but telling statement, far more powerful than a conceptual generalization, about the nature of the human condition: for is there a more intensely pertinent comment about mortality than the cessation of human habit, here identified with the nesting of swans but catalytic of so many other mortal cycles, open-ended in meaning yet specific and closed in the finality of its truth?

The swan was to occur as an image of ambiguity in a number of Yeats's most important poems. It was never an allegorical emblem but a metaphor for many states of meditation as in the case of all the other poets who wove their fiction around this figure. In the poem "Nineteen Nineteen" it identifies with the poet's labyrinth, substitution for his inner self. In that poem the swan is not fragile but wild, threatening, confronting darkness with a will to escape it. In spite of the fact that in his notes Yeats attributes his inspiration to Sturge Moore, a contemporary poet, it is remarkable for commentators to be so oblivious to the Symbolist movement and its predilection for swans as to attribute Yeats's attraction to the famous bird to past English poetry—in one case, indeed, to convoke Spenser. Every lake in Europe (and many lakes in America) was replete with swans at the time of Yeats as part of the *Anima Mundi* of his era, which he calls the "great pool" in his *Mythologies*.

In one of his most compelling poems, "The Tower," the swan recurs in a unique way. When Yeats makes his last testament in this poem and bequeaths his "pride," we must remember again that Mallarméan technique of substitutions. It is ap-

parent that the legacy of "pride" is his art, and his description
of pride/art is in terms of metaphors, not ideas, that convey the
effect of one thing on another ("the sudden shower / When all
streams are dry"), and when he wants to suggest the ephemeral
and its interface of mortality, the swan emerges this time as
suggestive of the "hour" pure and absolute in its autonomy:

> When the swan must fix his eye
> Upon a fading glean
> Float upon a long
> Last reach of glittering stream
> And there sing his last song

Against the fragility of the swan and its mortality he pits the
power of art beyond the grip of learned philosophers who create dialectics of "Death and life." Instead it is in his power as an
artist to create "Translunar Paradise."

In the Michael Robartes poems and "The Phases of the
Moon," several of the postsymbolist elements are prevalent,
particularly the notion of "verge" and in-between time; and the
image of the dancer seems here, as in the works of the other
poets grouped, the best qualified of the concrete forms of art to
suggest continuity and the passage of the creative artist into his
work.

"The Double Vision of Michael Robartes" follows very
closely the structure of Mallarmé's "Faun" in the interplay between mythological reality and poetic fiction. The standard
myth images are there in the form of the sphinx and a Buddha;
the girl dancing is the figment of the poet's imagination and/or
dream—a world of essences. There is the same uncertainty as in
Mallarmé's vision of the nymphs. Yet the fictitious appear "sol-
ider" as the artist's world is wrought in ethereal elements but
marked by permanence. But along with the poet's struggle to
overcome static mythology in superposing his ambiguous vision, the slippage is further stressed by certain nonconventional
notions of time, the in-between time/space from the old moon
to the new, and the more direct statement about overthrowing

time, a sine qua non of poetic fiction, to be even more brilliantly expressed in "Sailing to Byzantium." Here in the "Double Vision" it is not the division of the moon into phases that is the most illuminating factor but the space, the unnamed moment "When the old moon is vanished from the sky / And the new still hides her horn." In searching for the turning point or "verge" in Yeats, as I have been doing with the other poets involved in this study, one can alight on the two peaks of the "Phases of the Moon," the whole moon and the new, which correspond to Mallarmé's "Minuit absolu," his expression of the independence of that moment from temporal sequence. Yeats, on the other hand, less metaphysically expressive, declares it to be simply beyond the reach of Man.

It is only after that triumph over time, whether present or in antiquity, that the poet can turn the vision into song, which corresponds to Mallarmé's last line: renouncement of the mythological or dream experience for the "shadow," which, designated earlier in a familiar substitution of *painting* for *poems*, made the act of rape a breakthrough to poetic creation. The ambiguity of the "tu" at the end of Mallarmé's poem is produced by the fact that it has no antecedent and therefore no referential base. So, too, Yeats's poem of double vision is based not on the duality between an abstract ideal presented by the statues and a sensual one suggested by the dancing girls, but in the doubling he creates in the association of the girl with the past symbol of sensuality, even though she may be alive and they long dead, for it will be her fate to be dead. The real dichotomy lies between the "unremembering nights" (the dream) and turning into song, here associated with Homer (the work of art).

The art best qualified to suggest the amalgamation of the art with the artist is, as in Mallarmé, Valéry, and Rilke, the *dance*. Like them, Yeats loses the distinction between the performer and the performance. "How can we know the dancer from the dance?" he asks in "Among School Children," echoing, as it were, similar perceptions by the other poets mentioned above.

119

The metaphor of the dancer is manifest throughout Yeats's poetry. Again, as in the case of the swan, it is not an emblem but has the variability of the symbol. It may be the vision of a particular dancer—such as the well-known Loie Fuller, as was the easily identifiable Vera of Rilke. Or it is generalized as when Yeats observes, "All men are dancers." Most significantly of all, the dancer can be the embodiment of a philosophy.

The dichotomy between Robartes and the young dancer substantiates the struggle that inhabits Yeats as it does Valéry, Stevens, and Guillén: the conflict between philosophical poetry and a poetry that reflects an immanent philosophy in concrete image. In the Robartes poems the intrinsic knowledge or wisdom is embodied in the figure of the dancer. After evoking the Sphinx and Buddha emblems of philosophic revelation, he conjures the dancer: "And right between these two a girl at play /That, it may be, had danced her life away." In this particular poem—and let me again observe that this technique is not a sustained one in Yeats but powerful when it occurs—the dancing girl triumphs over intellect:

> O little did they care who danced between,
> And little she by whom her dance was seen
> So she had outdanced thought
> Body perfection brought,

The poet struggles in that in-between space and time, the moment of creation:

> Being caught between the pull
> Of the dark moon and the full

and

> Thereupon I made my moan,
> And after kissed a stone,
> And after that arranged it in a song.

Of course in the scheme of artistic interchanges, the song is the work of art, here the poem. But the questioning goes on in

"Robartes and the Dancer," and again in terms of a theological allusion Yeats confirms the greater power of the concrete, physical image over an abstract statement of thought.

Other collective symbols of the Zeitgeist utilized by Yeats to turn the real into the fiction of the poet are the tower and the gyre. They are remote from alleged inspirations of Shelley or Swedenborg. First, let Yeats speak for himself. In "Blood of the Moon" he explains:

> I declare this tower is my symbol. I declare
> This winding, gyring, spiring treadmill of a stair is my ancestral
>   stair.

In Symbolist meditation the tower and the ancestral stair to the personal catacombs are the outer limits of that wavering inner labyrinth that is projected onto the canvas of an enduring art. Both loci of contemplation for which Mallarmé substitutes in one of his most telling sonnets the cabinet of the Master facing the North Star, are sources of darkness and sudden illumination. Similarly, after the dialogue of "The Phases of the Moon," Yeats's poem ends with this cryptic comment: "The light of the tower window was put out." The gyre, Yeats's unique invention in the coterie of antipodal imagery, is a compelling and very physical metaphor of the vacillation between depth and height (azure in Mallarmé), which is the lot of the poet's sacerdotal function.

After having selectively collected evidences of Yeats's share in the symbolist *Anima Mundi*, let us proceed to the very poems that have received the most critical scrutiny—"The Second Coming," the Byzantium poems, and "Leda and the Swan." It is the most difficult to establish answers on the interpretation of these poems because they are the most cryptic and most directly in the morphological and conceptual context of the postsymbolist mode, which has virtually been overlooked in the study of Yeats. These poems have in common a structure that is both tight and open-ended—tight in form, open-ended in meaning. All can be read in terms of circumstantial, biographical, or historical data, but can be apprehended on a more universal plane as well. Whether they were meant to be read on a second level or not, all leave a semantic mystery for exegeses. But if they do not make complete sense as their interpreters have found, they make poetic sense on a conceptual basis— which is the distinction that the Symbolist theoreticians had as their objective in banishing both narrative and descriptive techniques. What primarily links these poems together is that they are all dominated by metaphoric language, which makes their philosophical message intrinsic rather than overt. Yeats, in fact, belies through his deft use of metaphor in these works the assumption of practitioners of hermeneutics that metaphor is only an emotive function of discourse and noninformative of our reality. As we know, Yeats wrote very often—in fact, most often—in direct, nonmetaphoric discourse, expressing ideas and emotions of both a personal and philosophical or political nature with images brought in as reinforcing devices.

When he departed from the more comfortable style, he must have done so consciously with the intention of reaching a more intricate form of his art. His use of metaphor in these poems is not limited to natural landscapes in opposition to human forms and functions. As pointed out earlier, he ventured, along with a whole generation of aesthetes, upon the use of known mythologies but deviating their meanings. This practice was a way of transcending both history and legend in the proclamation of the superiority of art, conceived as something beyond mythology or folklore.

Approaching "The Second Coming" as a larger metaphor than the one constricted to the historical context, we immediately become suspicious of the ready and obvious meaning of the title. I am not ignorant of the fact that this poem, written at a critical moment in history, comes to us with a heavy baggage of interpretations that take into account the state of the history of the Western world at the time of the writing of the poem. Yeats's own depressed state of mind over the fate of civilization, and also of the many previous models from Blake and Shelley, and from Gnosticism to Nietzsche, furbished his imagination. Without discounting these well-documented evidences, and remembering also that Mallarmé in a similar situation had at least fifty sources from which to derive his Hérodiade, I note what is absent here if it is to be taken as derivative of previous models. And knowing that Yeats was perfectly capable of writing a political poem, I wonder why he could not have done the same here if his purpose was to speculate on the dire future effects of the Russian Revolution. Or, in more direct allegory, he could well have created a Biblical apocalypse as so many of his revered predecessors had done.

Instead he chose the metaphoric, antihistorical approach in dealing with the larger issue of human failure, for indeed this is as powerful a poem about failure as Mallarmé's "Le vierge, le vivace et le bel aujourd'hui." Its applications are even larger. The initial image of the falcon and the falconer gives the immediate clue to what an artist most dreads in the execution of a work: the loss of control over its direction. There is the same image in Rilke's rider, where he conjures a second rider in the sky to bring the first one in line. Turning and turning suggests the effort, and we have already been told by Yeats that the gyre is the labyrinth of the self. Falconer as a substitution for artist is as legitimate as the many other substitutions we have seen in other symbolist poems. If the artist dreads his loss of control over his work, he also knows that when it happens he loses the unity of the work: "the center cannot hold." When control and unity are lost, art as well as the world are in a state of chaos. If with another substitution we consider "ceremony" to mean ritual, which according to Mallarmé applies to the work of art as much as to a religious service, and if "innocence" is purity, which is the ultimate objective of the artist as alchemist (that is, to render pure the reality full of mire and blood of human existence), then if the purity is not achieved, the failed work of art is "drowned" or destroyed.

When the artist reaches that level of failure he has but one hope—the second chance: for the redemption of the artist, the "second coming" is in that sense as crucial as for human welfare in general. So, he seeks new "revelation" or a new source of inspiration by plunging back into *Spiritu Mundi*, the treasure house of all symbols and indices.

The rest of the poem is so heavy with Biblical allusions that it is difficult to extricate it from the obvious context. Yet those who have tried to explain these allusions have found gross errors even when they have taken Blake's interpretation of the apocalypse as the point of departure or read the return of the Messiah in an ironic sense. Looking at the awesome vision from the purely aesthetic dimension, we know that after the dread of losing control and wrecking the unity of the artistic creation the thought most dreaded is the uncertainty of what may next emerge from the well of being and the unconscious state of the poet. As pointed out earlier, Mallarmé thought of the work of art as an operation as painful and as risky as giving birth, expressed in a poem that is one long metaphor: "Don du poème." In it the work of art is characterized as "Noire, a l'aile saignante et pale, déplumée" [Black with a bleeding and pale wing, deplumed], and he concluded by calling the birth of the poem "une horrible naissance."

Now, whether or not we conjecture that Yeats may have had this parallel of art and history in mind, the universal truth that metaphoric language adds to writing reveals that its applications are not only committed to those intended by the author; they also signal his poetic power to proliferate targets for the signifier. Is not all venture tinged with the fear of failure, and are not second chances even more terrifying in the renewed possibility of failure? For if it is a known adage that success breeds success, does not failure alert the victim of such failure beyond the hope of the second chance to the terror of a later monster in store for him? Such is the fate of civilizations, yes, but also of individuals in the miscarriage of their desires and efforts for fulfillment. Bethlehem, in the symbolist use of mythology, would be not only the birthplace of Christ but the birthplace of all new ventures, the rocking cradle the nurturing of such venture, and the expression "twenty centuries" in its metonymic sense is merely a historic delimitation in the context of eternity.

I have proposed that one of the ways the symbolists found to dispel from their work the deterministic chain of cause and effect prevalent in their time was by heightening the suspense of *waiting* as a defiance of certitude and inevitability. Alongside the "verge" element there is also that of the chance result that departs from the rationally expected effect of an action. The poem demonstrates these aspects of the human condition on a remarkably comprehensive level—not what one sensibly is entitled to expect, but what an uncontrollable chance may bring. The succinct poem, then, in this broad open-ended way, makes a statement not only on a circumstantial event (that is, on the Communist Revolution, as so many of Yeats's commentators believe) but on the nature of event itself, on the nature of human desire and the risks and perils it is heir to. The full power of symbolist *écriture* is thus demonstrated here.

In this same period, the two Byzantium poems can also be apprehended in symbolist dimensions. Commentators have speculated about the Byzantium reference in Yeats. Did he have in mind fourth-century Byzantium or the eleventh-century fall of the Byzantine empire? Again, there seems to be a consensus that the poetic inspiration comes through Shelley. But Yeats, much nearer to his contemporaries than to historical visions or the literary ones of Romanticism, was evoking the predominant fictitious space of European decadence. Byzantium had a symbolist meaning, codified by the time Yeats used it, which had all but dislodged it from its primary and historical one. The quality of Byzantium that the fin de siècle had crystallized was the notion of *fall*, the resplendent fatality of fall when it occurs from supreme height. The historical context that differentiated Byzantium from other political disasters was that its fall occurred at the peak of its power and opulence. Likewise, Europe had the sense of its own precipitous vulnerability at the moment of its highest flowering. So the analogy made prior to

125

Yeats's use of the term was no longer significant for his discovery of it but merely for his reference to it. Any originality, therefore, that he might have wanted to propose would have had to be on a new register rather than in conformance with the codified meaning of the decadent factor from which his generation had so deeply suffered.

Indeed, Yeats, like the Symbolists, had developed as part of his creative act the tendency to divert mythology from its accepted meaning and to add personal meaning to the collective symbols of his age. In this instance he banished the notion of fall in the midst of glory from the recognizable Byzantium image that had reached him, retaining it for its power both to have reached him and to have produced in the midst of its own perishable state the imperishable, unnatural form of human work we call by the name of art, which would survive political defeat. As painting, dancing, and music became substitutes in the naming of the poetic art in Mallarmé, Valéry, and Rilke, so Yeats, in the pure symbolist manner, avoided the word "poem" and focused his artistic objective on that form that makes the work of "Grecian goldsmiths" more durable than the most powerful emperor for whom they were fashioned. Their eternity is expressed in Yeats's own particular handling of non-measurable time. If in *Shadowy Waters* he uses the expression of outliving the moon, here the ending is expressed by simultaneity of past, present, and future: "to sing . . . / Of what is past, or passing, or to come." The artist singing of ephemeral things makes his work permanent by taking it out of historical context. Nowhere does Yeats come closer to Mallarmé in his concept of the role of the artist than in this poem. In his departure from nature, he asserts the triumph of the work of art over the perishable character of natural life, incorruptible in the face of corruptible nature and corruptible social structures. It survives over and above the artist, falconer, rider, and so on—all possible substitutions, including the sailor, headed for Byzantium. In the first two stanzas Yeats abandons all the phases of life inappropriate to the achievement of pure art: age, love, the guiles of natural beauty and its praise. Art is distinct from all levels and dominions of life that exist and are mortal. He suggests the great renunciation before sailing to Byzantium; the word "holy" has the significance of the sacred with which Mallarmé had endowed the arts.

Renunciation, sacrifice, purification are part of that ritual, that "ceremony of innocence" without which one may not reach the artifice of eternity. Mallarmé, while rejecting personal immortality, found great compensation in the fact that he was able to project that sense of immortality onto the work of art. So it is here, in the best of Yeats. After having sung on the lower register of praise and despair over mortal events he envisages the higher register of art that may escape the ravages of nature and of time. Art becomes then a liberation from nature. What Wallace Stevens was to call, in the wake of Mallarmé's earlier statement, "the supreme fiction" consists here in Yeats of gilded interiors of "golden bough."

I ventured to say in my reading of "The Second Coming" that the Biblical apocalypse that first comes to mind can be transcended; so also one can look beyond the historical Byzantium and see in the images of separation, distillation, sacrifice, by fire and torture, the steps of the ritual in the broader sense in which any venture toward the ideal is inherently the antithesis of the natural. The metaphor's self-contained wisdom carries its applications far beyond its rhetorical facade.

Certainly in Yeats's own poetry the metaphor is further elaborated in the course of the next three years and emerges in a poem equally terse albeit a little longer, called simply "Byzantium." Here Yeats's technique is even more apparent as he lets the concrete facts harbor something great and abstract. Whereas in the previous Byzantium poem he had begun with generalizations about the human condition and its frailties, this time he has carried over the crystallized image with which he ended the earlier poem, thus giving the two poems a certain continuity, semantic as well as referential. Here the ceremony of purification is to be carried to a higher intensity since Byzantium itself is submitted to it: it is no longer a goal but a point of departure in the quest.

"The unpurged images" are a sly, subtle reference to the earlier "ceremony of innocence." The images of recession multiply, involving human nature as the purging leaves behind a cosmos disdainful of man. The metonymies of fury and mire and the abstract notion tied into the concrete material, both catalytic to the vision of the human, are further degraded by the normally unacceptable alliance of "mere" with "complexities." Human pride in human complexities is thus minimized and leveled off, preparing the way for the first nonmetaphoric statement: "I hail the superman." The important thing here is that although at the time of Yeats and thereafter the superman was to be associated with Nietzschean philosophy, the context in which Yeats uses the term is aesthetic and not heroic or epistemological: the miracle that is suggested in the next stanza is of artistic permanence and not mythically divine. It is a degree even beyond the permanence of gold, which was the level of significance in the previous Byzantium poem.

The last stanza is situated in absolute time, the magical midnight. What Mallarmé called "Minuit absolu" in *Igitur* as his Orphic exploration of the ancestral abyss becomes the familiar approximation in Yeats's own turning gyre. The negative elements in the stanza qualifying the positive realities precipitate these toward death. But, like Rilke's "Vergens im Gang," the dying is absolved into art (that is, the dance), and in the transformation even the flame, delivered of its physical properties, has submitted to the ceremony of innocence (that is, the alchemy of the artist), and it is now incapable of functioning in conventional fashion, as, for instance, to "singe a sleeve." After the image of fire there is a series of images of rupture suggesting the total extraction of all that is contaminated with the human or its water-equivalent, the dolphin, and the more radical operation that suggests the clean sweep: "Those images that yet fresh images beget." It consists of an endless revolution that deconstructs, with torn and tormented effects, phonemically synchronizing all destructive action in the perilous adventure of the all-englobing artist.

This poem is perhaps the most powerful of all the poetry of Yeats concerning the power of art; it is as if the whole universe were cooperating to deliver the artist from all human problems, physical and psychological, in order for him to exercise his creative activity. Whereas the previous poem is a serene one, this one is dynamic: it is a purgative holocaust for a still newer substitution for the artist in the guise of "the golden smithies of the Emperor," whose handiwork is the miracle of the golden bird "Planted on the star-lit golden bough":

> . . . . scorn aloud
> In glory of changeless metal
> Common bird or petal
> And all complexities of mire and blood.

The gold and marble transcend the everlasting cycle of earthly perils: "That dolphin-torn, that gong-tormented sea." The gong forewarns of the storms of nature but the gilded palace that it surrounds remains untouched, presumably even as the work of the artist is saved.

From the point of view of symbolist aesthetics, the most successful of Yeats's poems is in my opinion "Leda and the Swan." As I have long maintained, it would have been impossible for Yeats to have ignored the swan symbol in the age in which he lived since it was the very signature of a universal poetic identity in its culture. Allusions here and there, as we have observed, would not have sufficed without having done a "swan poem" of his own, transcending the stereotypes. Earlier, in the treatment of the swan image in *The Wild Swans at Coole*, he gave it a dream function. In continental European poetry swan poems had two levels of usefulness—as dream triggers and as associations with poetic states of mind. No two poets used the swan code in quite the same manner. In Baudelaire it begot a long list of mnemonic associations of states of alienation to which legendary and real humans are subjected in exile; in Mallarmé it became a symbol of purity to which the poet aspired but could not attain. Yeats's treatment in "Leda and the Swan" goes more in the direction of Rilke, who saw in the coitus of Jupiter with Leda the infusion of the divine into the human and, in that sense, an aesthetic operation (poetry created by the junction of human perception and the divine transformation of it). Yeats added the dimension of "will" to the penetration in the belief that random association of the sacred and the corporeal will not produce art; conception occurs only when the poet is further strengthened by the will—that is, the conscious craft of the artist alone makes the masterpiece possible.

Here, as in some other poems of Yeats, the function of historical facts was expanded to reflect on the broader and more pervasive problems of the human condition or on the plight of the artist. Thereby the myth as metaphor, rather than as a psychological symbol, is infinitely variable in its applications to a vaster spectrum of human concerns. In the most terse and yet vivid verbal reconstruction of rape, the poem is reminiscent of Mallarmé's *Afternoon of a Faun*. Whereas the faun's attack on the nymphs was identified as a "morsure" [bite], here it is a blow, suggestive of extreme power and in compliance with Mallarmé's dictum to the poet: to search the effect of one entity on another. The thunder is Jupiter in the guise of a swan, again expressed only by the metonymies of wing, web, and feather; the forest or receiver is suggested by the metonymies of thighs, nape, breast, fingers of resistance, and the effect is first suggested by the shudder. And had it stopped there the poem would have been a strikingly symbolist exercise. But the symbolism has a much larger implication. In illustrating his challenge to historical event—that is, the fall of Troy—Yeats takes a nonsequential view of it and extends the impact of the individual act to the vaster problems of the human condition that it can be found to imply.

The correspondence between the willed and the chance event is one of the highest mysteries of life, and Yeats involves that mystery in his treatment of the rape of Leda and its disastrous consequences. He engages the reader in the question of the interplay between liberty and chance. The signifiers "knowledge" and "power" are pitted against the "indifferent beak." The disproportion between the micro-action of the swan and the macro-catastrophe of historical event is but an index to the infinite, open-ended parallels both on the personal level and on the universal one that the metaphor encompasses. The fantasy of Jupiter will produce the love child Helen, who will unwittingly cause the war and the fall of Troy. Or did Jupiter willfully create Helen as the agent of that historical disaster? On the political level one might go so far as to say that the passivity or supine nonengagement of Leda is also a form of engagement. Lack of sufficient resistance can be perceived as a form of cooperation. So flexible is the metaphor of this myth that Hispano-American poets used the rape of Leda as an image of Jupiter-imperialism in relation to the European colonization of America.

Yeats in these powerful and succinct poems joins Mallarmé, Valéry, and Rilke in tackling the most legitimate and crucial of the concerns of symbolist poets: the universal lottery in which human beings engage when they pit their will (in life as in art) against the indifferent but overwhelming forces of chance.

As in his Dialogue, there are in Yeats's poetry two voices—that of the self and that of the soul—running parallel to Valéry's *Animus* and *Anima*, and in Rilke to the sculptured permanence of reality and the floating ambiguity of his uninterpretable world. The self in Yeats is engaged in the historical moments of his time; the soul is affixed to the Emperor's palace, on the open sea, in the phases of the moon—spaces prohibited to the ordinary living man in the unresolved battle between the demolitionary powers of chance and the sometimes equally tragic consequences of the free exercise of human will and its self-generated fatalities. The very fact that poets without theological commitments write about the struggle with chance instead of resorting to a stoical silence shows the high stakes they accept in the elaboration of the work of art.

Fifty years after his death, a consensus among Yeats scholars has established him as the direct heir of Blake and Shelley, and he has been read mostly in the context of the Romantic tradition. Yeats is thus heavily laden with an intertextuality that defines him as a postromantic. Would it not be more appropriate to link him with poets chronologically closer to him if a bit more distant nationally, who shared with him the experience of "the trembling of the veil"? In the mosaic of his work, the postsymbolist mode I have highlighted is one of the prevalent patterns he received and transmuted. They lent a universal meaning to his primordial concerns over the frailty and strength of human destiny and its expression in the arts.

Stevens and the Symbolist Mode

IF THERE ARE thirteen ways of looking at a blackbird, there must be at least a hundred ways of looking at Wallace Stevens. A poet's poet as well as a scholar's, he penetrated more than fifty years (d. 1955) into the twentieth century, and in its closing decade has assumed for many readers and critics the role of the top-ranking American poet of the century. Any scholar of Anglo-American literature would want to do—and has, in most cases, done—an interpretation of Stevens just as any musician would test his interpretive and musical skills with a performance of Beethoven or Paganini. For a violinist, the technical difficulty of Paganini's works would be the ultimate test of the performer's own craftsmanship. So it is with readings of Stevens. As a critical writer, I have not written on American poetry except in the contribution of two introductions to two successive reprints of my book on surrealism.[1] In these I have been critical of contemporary American poetry. It may therefore be an affront to my numerous predecessors to tread on the sacred ground of Stevens scholarship, and by way of justifying my rites of passage I hasten to note that whereas the bulk of Stevens's work is much more extensive than that of most of the other poets included in this particular reading, I am, as I explained in the case of Rilke and Yeats, concerned with only a slice of his writings. But in this case there is a difference: the other poets were treated sectionally, whereas here the symbolist mode is not a chronological part of the progressive work, situating an aspect of it. In my probing of Stevens I am pursuing a "vein" that prevails throughout the work and is an element that contrasts with the rest of the work, reflecting a

---

[1] *Surrealism: The Road to the Absolute* (Chicago, 1987).

curious aspect of his character that does not quite fit into the general pattern of his life.

One of the paradoxical problems that confront such a study is the explicitly national quality of Stevens. Whereas the others included here in the legacy of Mallarmé had a cosmopolitan facet to their career or work (even Yeats was bicultural and had traveled abroad), Stevens's lifestyle was what used to be called "isolationist"—not politically but circumstantially; financial reasons prevented him from taking even a tourist's trip to Europe. His closest foreign contact probably came from attending Harvard and living for a while in Greenwich Village. But his traveling was done through books, and France is part of it, even on the superficial level of his practice of dropping French words and French titles throughout the corpus of his writings.

A larger problem looms. There are so many American poets of the 1920s and 1930s whose symbolist connection has already been identified and who would presumably fit better into the current mosaic that one might well ask, "why pick Stevens?" To clear that perplexity, it has to be realized that symbolist influence is not necessarily postsymbolist manifestation.

In general, when the impact of French Symbolism on American poets is acknowledged,[2] the recipients are found in the American school called "imagism." One of the best-known of these writers on Symbolism is Amy Lowell, who, in her book *Six Poets*, discussed Emile Verhaeren, Albert Samain, Remy de Gourmont, Henri de Regnier, Francis Jammes, and Paul Fort. The first four of these were integrally part of the Symbolist *cénacle*; the last two inhabited the Symbolist ambience by association and were labeled by the first historians of the major movement of the epoch as "Symbolists."

[2] Rene Taupin's *L'influence du Symbolisme français su la poésie americaine de 1910–1912* (Paris, 1929) has become a classic on the subject and is unsurpassed in its delimitations. Translated in the AMS edition (New York, 1987), it is a rich sourcebook. See also Haskell Block, "The Impact of French Symbolism on Modern American Poetry," in *The Shaken Realist* (Baton Rouge, 1970). On Stevens, see Michel Benamou, *Wallace Stevens and the Symbolist Imagination* (Princeton, 1972).

The last two are homely poets in the English sense of the word; Fort enveloped himself in rhythm and legend, and Jammes enclosed himself in an intimate natural landscape, rustic and anthropocentric. Both tend toward eloquence in a rather direct form of discourse and neither is aware of the need to signify in poetry ontological readjustments. The first four on Amy Lowell's list are typical, and representative of the host of poets who assimilated the tropes cultivated by the Symbolists. They perfected, varied, and developed the images resulting from the powerhouse of anguish bequeathed to them by Baudelaire, Rimbaud, and Mallarmé. But they did not rethink for themselves the scenario of the anguish, the power of rejection that produced the wasteland from which artificially grew a new crop of poetry. Gourmont, as a naturalist novelist and eminent critic, did much to promote the other three on the list as the exemplary models of Symbolism.

They were letter-perfect in their cultivation of fog and uncertainty (Verhaeren) or in restoring the Hellenic world as a base for the poetic imagination (Regnier). In polished verse they evoked facsimiles of Hérodiades, swans, castles, flowers, and all the immediately recognizable images of Symbolism. They turned Symbolism into a form of neoclassicism, and it is this form of the symbolist imprint that was imported to the United States—not the tortuous, skeptical, iconoclastic use of language that became the veil of meaning after Mallarmé made the known veils separating reality from the fictions of the artist tremble.

It has already been noted that the greatness of Symbolism as Mallarmé manifested it slipped out of France on two levels—as imitation and as transformation. In the United States, the imitative character was reinforced by the fact that in 1900 Henri de Regnier came to Harvard as Visiting Professor of Romance Languages; there he had T. S. Eliot as a student, and his work came to be viewed in Cambridge's poetic circles as a model of polished verse. He and, by association, his coterie were readily accepted by the people around *Poetry* magazine under the leadership of Harriet Monroe, who aimed "to attain in English certain subtleties of cadence of the kind which Mallarmé and his followers have studied in French." Analyzing this sentence we see that *cadence*, or *a sequence of sound* in music, is the focus of the interest, and although the name of Mallarmé is mentioned, his followers are the active practitioners of Symbolist poetry.

The following poem of Walter Conrad Arensberg shows how well the author has learned his lesson:[3]

> The swan existing
> Is like a song with an accompaniment
> Imaginary
>
> Across the glassy lake;
> Across the lake to the shadow of the willows
> It is accompanied by an image
>
> As by Debussy's
> "Reflet dans l'eau"
>
> The swan that it
> Reflects
> Upon the solitary water breast to breast
> With the duplicity
> "The other one!"
>
> And breast to breast it is confused.
> A visionary wedding! O stateliness of the procession!
>
> It is accompanied by the image itself
> Alone
>
> At night
> The lake is a wide silence
> Without imagination.

The ingredients are all there: the swan, music, narcissism, shadow, lake, mirror effect, the silent indifference of nature

---

[3] Walter Conrad Arensberg, "Voyage à l'Infini," in *Idols* (Boston, 1916), 12–13.

when the poet's power of mediation is withdrawn. Even Rimbaud's "je est un autre" is thrown in. It is a neat assimilation, the natural reflection of sad swan onto even more listless water, reinforced by a reference to Debussy's work in an impressionistic suggestion of the movement of water and willow. Lacking are the more sophisticated interstices of Valéry's handling of the Narcissus legend, the slipping in of the factor of transformation occurring in the mirror image; also missing is the duplicity of Rilke's *Doppelreich*, the alchemical operation that makes "the other" not a substitute or projection but a denser replacement and a new creation. The deeper tradition that Mallarmé launched is not there. And the hyperboles that Symbolism was supposed to have eliminated reenter the poetic discourse.

When another poet, John Gould Fletcher, inspired by the French Symbolists, read the following stanza to Amy Lowell, the latter exclaimed, "Why, my dear boy, you have genius":

> The spattering of the rain upon pale terraces
> Of afternoon is like the passing of a dream
> Amid the roses shuddering 'gainst the wet stalks
> Of the streaming trees . . .

But Fletcher was candid enough to attribute his power of creating metaphor to the lessons he had learned from the French poets: "You will find if you read Baudelaire, Mallarmé, Verlaine, Rimbaud, Verhaeren carefully, that I am not so original as you think." Of the five poets he mentioned, it is obvious that the one who affected him most was Verlaine.

In the case of Allen Tate there is a double tier of indoctrination. On the one hand, he indulges to the point of distraction in a medley of metaphors coupling abstract thought with concrete images, and on the other, he misreads Baudelaire's theory of correspondences by connecting Baudelaire with medieval metaphysical poetics. An essay, "The Fugitive," dated 1924, tells the reader: "Today the poet's vocabulary is prodigious, it embraces the entire range of consciousness—that an idea out of one class of experience may be dressed up in the vocabulary of another is at once the backbone of modern poetic diction and the character which distinguishes it from both the English tradition and free verse." In another essay, "The Symbolic Imagination," he leads the reader farther down the erroneous path by saying, "the symbolic imagination conducts an action by analogy, of the human and the divine, of the natural to the supernatural, of the low to the high, of time to eternity. My generation was deeply impressed by Baudelaire's sonnet, 'Correspondences,' which restated the doctrines of medieval symbolism by way of historical perspective leading back to the original source."

Tate's misreadings of Symbolism are important because, as a leading poet of his era, he was much emulated, and he prompted a style of antiseptic poetry from which American poetry was not liberated until the advent of the garish earthiness of the poets of post–World War II. Where Baudelaire had used Swedenborg's dictum the better to reject it subtly, the faulty translation of certain expressions such as "expansion des choses infinies" and "les transports de l'esprit et des sens" brought him right back in line with Swedenborg's conception of the teleological duality of the universe. The fact that Baudelaire and after him Mallarmé had thought of language as something other than "dressing" did not penetrate the translations. Above all, showing this duality to be the exact opposite of the English tradition does gross negligence to England's metaphysical poets who should have been, rather than Baudelaire, the target of Tate's reference. Where Mallarmé was trying to replace the theological dichotomy by a new one between nature and the artist's fiction, Tate turned the innovative perception into a revival of medieval symbolism, leading totally astray those American poets who looked up to him as a theoretician. There followed several decades of warmed-over, stereotyped poetry, elegant in its perfection of models derived from mistranslations from the French.

It is also interesting to note that in this period of static pro-liferation the powerful poets of the neosymbolist group, high-lighted here, did not enjoy much literary recognition in the United States. Valéry was not yet officially translated, nor was Rilke; and Yeats was overshadowed by T. S. Eliot, Pound, Joyce, and D. H. Lawrence.

Ezra Pound did not do much to correct the misinterpreta-tions of the Symbolist aesthetics. A remarkable virtuoso in the use of lexicons in the manner of his French counterpart, Théophile Gautier, Pound was outside the battle for the expan-sion of the poetic field: the development of an idiom to express the grave ontological deviation of the time, the struggle with language that had been too strictly tailored to reflect a previous perception of the universe. Pound's skills and gifts lay else-where; he was creating a new rhetoric, multiplying words or positioning them in intricate syntax instead of decomposing them or expanding their range, or even pulverizing them as French poets were successively doing.

Another poet was lurking behind the eloquent imitators of the Symbolists: more in the spirit of the initiator, Mallarmé, than of the rank and file of the Symbolist school, Wallace Ste-vens apparently led a well-ordered life consisting of the stan-dard progression from university studies to marriage, and steady employment that eventually led him to become an insur-ance man in Hartford, Connecticut. He was in his lifestyle comparable to Mallarmé, schoolteacher of Tournon, who was eventually promoted to a Paris appointment.

Stevens, like Mallarmé, reshuffled the world's dichotomies so that the separation is not between heaven and earth but be-tween uncontrollable powers of the material world and the sphere of the poet's control. Also, like Mallarmé, he separated the need to earn a livelihood from that part of his life involved in poetic experience. Rilke could wield "Sein"/"Dasein" and Jorge Guillén "ser"/"estar" to express the distinction between an existence that measures time in chronos and one that relates

139

to kairos or intensive time periods through the subtleties of their respective languages. Stevens, saddled like Mallarmé with a language that did not provide through its lexicon a built-in semantic difference, had to create it by linguistic circumventions. Even as someone with a physical handicap is often challenged to develop greater manipulative maneuvers, so the linguistic shortcomings were in this respect to lead Mallarmé and subsequently Wallace Stevens to literary tours de force and virtuosity of poetic rendering in their native tongues.

Early in his career Stevens took up Mallarmé's notion that poetry was a form of fiction created through a sophisticated use of language, and he eventually made this concept the basis of his poetic theory as crystallized in his long poem *Notes toward a Supreme Fiction*.

But before entering into a detailed analysis of Stevens, which departs, as in the case of my approach to Yeats and Rilke, from the conventional one based on national lineage, the theory of cross-national influence may well be pondered. Stevens has been known to say, "The great source of modern poetics is probably France." On the other hand, when questioned about the impact of Mallarmé on him, he has specifically denied any direct influence: "Mallarmé never in the world meant as much to me as all that in any direct way. Perhaps I absorbed more than I thought. Mallarmé was a good deal in the air when I was much younger. But so were other people, for instance Samain. Verlaine meant a good deal more to me. There were many of his lines that I delighted to repeat. But I was never a student of any of these poets; they were simply poets and I was the youthful general reader" (*Correspondences*, 636).

Yet in what is one of the best books written about Stevens, *L'Oeuvre-Monde de Wallace Stevens*, the late Michel Benamou gives concrete textual proof of an anatomical resemblance that is hard to attribute to mere coincidence. Above all, it becomes undeniable in the framework of the era that the philosophy implicit in this poetry can be associated with a general Zeitgeist representative of those shedding the anthropocentric universe.

As a substitute for a human world accepted by us collectively, there emerges a poetic pretense to create a personal one. This attribute encourages the notion of the fiction of poetry, the function of language to serve this fiction, the posture of the poet as a priestly mediator, creating an association not only with Mallarmé but with certain others of his generation. This associative power places Mallarmé at the center not of a school—where students may learn by rote, and perhaps too well to be original themselves—but of a radiation that mutates and transforms those who partake of its source of energy. Without this conscious or unconscious emulation of Mallarmé, Stevens would have adhered more closely to general American poetic trends of the moment. Instead, looking back on the century, we see him stand out like the hill among the monotonous valleys to borrow the metaphor by which Guillaume Apollinaire describes all innovators in his prophetic poem "Les Collines."

If a parallel may be drawn, André Breton, a leader of another mode of poetic *écriture*, surrealism, diligently named his models, including Freud, but omitted Dr. Pierre Janet, the psychiatrist in whose writings he had gleaned, as I discovered, the most pointed words and underlying concepts of his poetic theory.[4] Is it not an unwitting rejection of what is feared to be an influence? But as Harold Bloom puts it so well in his *Poetry and Repression*, poetry is a series of reactions to other previous poetry, and without this process of interpretation of one poet by another, which is at the heart of the process we call "influence," we cannot note the manner of substitution that each great poet makes to his interpretation of another, and that is the surest gauge of his originality as opposed to what is in a not-so-great poet simple imitation.

Such is the status of Stevens vis-à-vis Symbolism, in contrast to what an imagist poet directly appropriates, often as a result

---

[4] Pierre Janet, *L'Automatisme psychologique*, 9th ed. (Paris, 1921), and *De l'Angoisse à l'Extase* (Paris, 1926).

of an unintentional misreading of the original, as noted in the case of Allen Tate. But where Bloom's methodology is applied to the English strain of Stevens, the cross-national is here presented as the more significant one because, as in most such cases, I have observed that the attraction is more catalytic when it passes from one national literature to another than when it remains within a single one. The concern here, then, is what Stevens took consciously or unconsciously from Mallarmé and returned alchemically to the collective consciousness of the function and destiny of poetry in the post-apocalyptic world.

Where Harold Bloom attributes Stevens's ontology to readings of Emerson, Nietzsche, and Schopenhauer, which would make Valéry a simultaneous recipient of this same wisdom, it is a detour that can be avoided if we see Stevens and Valéry appropriating an already modified philosophy from Mallarmé. At least in the major poems of Stevens the source and its derivation are clearly Mallarméan. If it is true that Stevens was troubled about the idea of influence, it is, just the same, more logical to associate him with poets than with Freud or nihilist philosophers.

An early work, "Le Monocle de mon Oncle," clearly reveals certain clues. Why the French? It comes back again in *L'Esthétique du mal*. Is the transfer of language not part of the fiction he is looking for, more acceptable in the guise of a foreign language than in the earthy one associated with man's daily reality?

In learning a foreign language one memorizes artificially constructed expressions, one of the most absurd of which has been known to be "le parapluie de mon oncle." Stevens is obviously showing the irrelevance of practicality to the structure of language, but in designating the irrelevance he is focusing on "monocle," which is a reference to vision, but a partial one: is this not a deviation from total reality, just as the structure of the expression, correct in syntax, has nothing to tell us of practical value? The theme in this poem is the cyclic return of the seasons, a subject well worn out, a little reminiscent of Yeats's

142

The Wild Swans at Coole. Here it is the firefly and the cricket that remind the poet of the ticking away of time—all very Romantic, one might say, except that at the center of the poem, the poet is no longer being dragged through the cycle by outside forces. Instead, he is tying it all together into a synthesis of art, through a central color and a superposition of the imagined tree over the real one.

However monocular the vision, it is better than two clear eyes facing minimal reality. He is shaking that "bond to all that dust," which the crickets first brought to his attention through their return to a death synchronic with that of humans. The stanza that follows finds the poet rejecting that condition just as surely as Mallarmé's Faun rejected his failure to catch the nymphs:

> If men at forty will be painting lakes
> The ephemeral blues must merge for them in one,
> The basic slate, the universal hue.
> There is a substance in us that prevails . . .
> It is a theme for Hyacinth alone.

The reference to Hyacinth, like Valéry's Narcissus and Rilke's Daphne, makes it more suggestive of the power of transformation of something dead into something ever-living. The theme of Hyacinth is similar to the theme of the Syrinx, whereby the ephemeral (reed/flower) is transformed into an eternal provocation for artistic and nonephemeral creation.

Coming to the tree symbol so dear to Rilke, Stevens turns the tables on nature. As a result, nature imitates the poet's concept, whereas man is expected to imitate nature:

> But, after all, I know a tree that bears
> A semblance to the thing I have in mind

In *The Man with the Blue Guitar*, whose very title is a successful synaesthesia of sound and color, the unifying power of color observable in "The Monocle" is joined by the even more englobing one of music. The unimportance of subject matter is central to the poem, which is at the same time process and self-contained subject:

> Poetry is the subject of the poem
> From this the poem issues and
>
> To this returns. Between the two
> Between issue and return
>
> An absence in reality
> Things as they are. Or so we say.
>
> ("Le Monocle," stanza 22)

In this context Bloom's explanation of Stevens's notion of the invented world is misleading. He says, "From Vaihiinger-on-Nietzsche, Stevens took the idea of this invention, the invented world, and more crucially even, the notion that the world in which we lived was itself a fiction, just as our autonomous self or identity was only a fiction or a 'supreme fiction.'"[5] Clearly this is not what Stevens is suggesting either here, or, as we shall see, in *Notes toward a Supreme Fiction*. For Mallarmé and for those who followed him the fiction is the only reality and what is outside is absence of that reality created by the poet. But this created or invented reality cannot be called "illusion" because it is the only one that survives, as we have already observed in Mallarmé. The poet is no longer dealing with correspondences or mediations but with direct takeover, invasion, incrustation: "the lion and the lute" is the poet speaking through music; "the lion locked in stone" is the inscription/poem having the durability of stone. The stone image is more clearly defined in the long poem *Rock*, which will be discussed presently in a larger context. Like Mallarmé, Stevens warns the reader/fellow poet not to name things—"Do not use rotted names"—and, just as in Stevens's case the theory of poetry is often incorporated in the poem itself, *The Man with the Blue Guitar* is an "art poétique" as well as its demonstration:

[5] Harold Bloom, *Poetry and Repression* (n.p., n.d.), 281.

Nothing must stand
Between you and the shapes you take
When the crust of shape has been destroyed

Renaming or suggesting is not enough for Stevens; he destroys shapes as well, replacing them with tonality or hue. In his own way he is groping toward "la notion pure" of objects.

Music is one of the transformers. The man with the blue guitar is a humble sort of Orpheus, but his power is not the less. "Things as they are / are changed upon the blue guitar." Humbly he "patches" the world. If movement and change are signets of life as it is, then things that music places "beyond the compass of change / Perceived in a final atmosphere" are signets of art. And amid that indifference that is the sea or sun, the artist is "The maker of a thing yet to be made."

It is obvious that Stevens attributed to music a superior place among the arts since he gave two of his most important collections musical titles—*Harmonium* and *The Man with the Blue Guitar*. But unlike the standard Symbolist, he did not imitate in verse the sound and resonance of music as did Verlaine, René Ghil, and all the other Instrumentalists that followed them; instead, like Mallarmé, he placed poetry above music as the substitution for religious transcendence and, like Mallarmé, assumed for the poet the sacerdotal function in *The Man with the Blue Guitar*:

Poetry
Exceeding music must take the place
Of empty heaven and its hymns

Later in the poem, the poet/musician/priest is in the "self" that incorporates the soul:

A substitute for all the gods;
This self, not that gold self aloft

If music is a creative element, so is color. Like Mallarmé, Stevens suggests the work of the poet through that of the painter as well as that of the musician in a process of substitution and identification of all artists for one another. In the first stanza the day was green. Stevens describes the function of color; the lines "And the color like a thought that grows / Out of a mood" imply that color is no more intrinsic to things than is sound, but it is part of the fiction of the artist, as in what he calls "true appearances" and "sun's green / Cloud's red."

Yet, whether with color or sound, the poet/painter/musician does not have the same stature as for Mallarmé. At one moment Stevens imagines a godlike hero, reminiscent of Chonchoru, the Indian chieftain who is said to have retreated to the top of the mountain and then jumped to his death in a fit of insanity. But in general he settles for a more modest model. The poet is not conceived in the guise of the high priest, as in the case of Mallarmé, but as having a more lowly stature, somewhat reminiscent of the tobacco smoker of Ruben Dario's "Sinfonia en gris major."

The images that the blue guitar evokes are humble and cosmic at the same time, and soon the two images of the lofty and the lowly merge in a melded image "A poem like a missal found / In the mud, a missal for that young man." The difference lies in the fact that "the old fantoche" with whom Stevens finally identifies is as far from the priestly demeanor as the missal in the mire is from the *Livre* to which Mallarmé aspired. If for both poets the work of art is a fiction of an invented world, Wallace Stevens's has a closer parallel with Oxidia, or local space, and the music slips between things as they are, making the reader realize that the blue guitar asserts the imagined— "The moments when we choose to play / The imagined pine, the imagined jay"—but does not evoke it in any stylized form in the closing lines of the long poem.

Often Stevens employs birds not as intermediaries between heaven and earth, as other poets are wont to do, but as the accomplices of the creative self. And, like Mallarmé, he strips the sky of the denotation of heaven. This struggle with "ciel" was more of a theoretical problem for Mallarmé, one would imag-

ine, since in French the same word carries both the physical and
the material meaning. It was with the metaphoric meaning of
"azur" that he struggled to divest it of its supernal meaning.
But where one would imagine Stevens's job to be easier in distinguishing lexically the signifiers "heaven" and "sky," the need
to see above him nothing but the blue is so pressing that the
word "Blue" becomes suspect and he desymbolizes the color by
using a less common denotation, "indigo," in *The Man with the
Blue Guitar* to designate the sphere above. It is the same kind
of evasion and distortion of "ciel" as in Mallarmé's use of
"azur." The severance from eternal divinities becomes central
and even more explicit in *Notes toward a Supreme Fiction*, as we
shall see.

In another self-portrait in substitution, this time with a rebellious spirit that reminds us of Rimbaud, "Landscape with
Boat" describes the poet as "An anti-master-man, floribund ascetic," which suggests the paradox of a productive ascetic, combining the static posture with movement. What follows carries
through the theme of the rebellious destructor as in *A Season in
Hell* of Rimbaud, where he said, "I tore from the sky / heaven
its azure which is blackness and I lived, a spark of gold in light
in its natural form." The same effect of ripping the natural
world is experienced in Stevens's poem:

> He brushed away the thunder, then the clouds,
> Then the colossal illusion of heaven. Yet still
> The sky was blue. He wanted imperceptible air.
> He wanted to see. He wanted the eye to see
> And not be touched by blue. He wanted to know
> A naked man who regarded himself in the glass
> Of air, who looked for the world beneath the blue,
> Without blue, without any turquoise tint or phase,
> Any azure under-side or after-color. Nabob
> Of bones, he rejected, he denied, to arrive
> At the neutral centre, the ominous element,
> The single-colored, colorless, primitive.

147

The revelation in the case of Stevens is not as illuminating as in Rimbaud's "Lumiere *nature*." "Yet still the sky was blue," as he says: the empty or black character of the denoted blue is not as easily chased as in Rimbaud's. Or perhaps it can even be said that Stevens is older and wiser and does not believe in ready miracles. The need for an unveiling of the blue accommodates at the end of the poem to "the emerald of the Mediterranean."

The central poem encompassing aesthetic theory in Stevens is undoubtedly *Notes toward a Supreme Fiction*. Even as for Mallarmé[6] poetry was the pure fiction, and for Rilke a rejection of the interpreted world, so in this poem the concept of poetic discourse is blatantly denoted by "this invented world." It is a tearing-away process on a larger scale than in "Landscape with Boat." To invent is to become ignorant of the central force of the sun and to focus on "the idea of it"—"notion pure," as Mallarmé had said:

> How clean the sun when seen in its idea
> Washed in the remotest cleanliness of a heaven
> That has expelled us and our images . . .
> The death of one god is the death of all

The one god he refers to is of course the sun god, Phoebus, yet here Stevens is erasing not only the existence of the god but the possibility of the verbalization of the concept: "But Phoebus was / A name for something that never could be named." The implication is that the power to name precedes the power to exist (as in the Genesis), and destruction of the concept cannot occur without destruction of the naming. If the poet is an architect, which seems to be the identification evoked this time by Stevens through his reference to Viollet-le-Duc, the first step in displacement and substitution does in fact carry the

---

[6] Helen Vendler, in *On Extended Wings* (Cambridge, Mass., 1969), examines *Notes* closely and calls it "the most harmonious expression of Stevens's late flowering genius," but makes no reference to the notion of fiction in relation to poetry, which resonates with Mallarmé so clearly.

double operation. So, indeed, is the description of vision—"A seeing and unseeing in the eye."

The supreme fiction occurs as he tells us when things and phenomena regain their pristine integrity, losing the layers and layers of meaning they have gathered like dust. Artifice occurs when vision is emptied of previous representations and interpretions of objects, figures, landscapes, and seascapes.

Again in this poem music is the unifying force, "a will to change," the steadying reliable element in a world that the poet considers plagued with "inconstancy." When in the midst of theoretical assertions Stevens gives glimpses of the invented universe, it is wrought with misplaced colors:

> On a blue island in a sky-wide water
> . . . A green baked greener in the greenest sun.

or,

> The water of the lake was full of artificial things
> That is how we made the world our own.

The word "artificial" is used in the Mallarméan sense of a creative fiction denying natural realities. As Mallarmé's Faun conjured "the visible and serene artificial breath / Of inspiration, which reconquers the sky/heaven," Mallarmé's declaration of man's colonization of the divine place by art is reechoed in Stevens's definition of the supreme fiction. It is a poetic and not a philosophical conquest, replete with all the inconsistencies, uncertainties, and irrationalities that constitute the charm of poetry.

> A bench was his catalepsy. Theatre
> Of trope. He sat in the park. The water of
> The lake was full of artificial things.
>
> Like a page of music, like an upper air
> Like a momentary color, in which swans
> Were seraphs, were saints, were changing essences.

The purity of the poem is expressed, as in Mallarmé, in the concept of "essence," and exists like a soul before being even named: "Is there a poem that never reaches words?"

As Stevens defines the power of the poet it is "to catch from that irrational moment its unreasoning." A series of images are interspersed between the theoretical assertions.

> A lasting visage in a lasting bush,
> A face of stone in an unending red,
> Red-emerald, red-slitted-blue, a face of slate

Again, here the mismatching of colors is one of the effective ways in which Stevens suggests the artificial.

The power of synaesthesia comes again to his aid to suggest the interception of the senses of sight and hearing as the junction of illumination.

> Beneath, far beneath, the surface of
> His eye and audible in the mountain of
> His ear, the very material of his mind

The purpose of the creative art is

> to find the real
> To be stripped of every fiction except one
> The fiction of an absolute—Angel
> Be silent in your luminous cloud and hear
> The luminous melody of proper sound . . . I can
> Do all that angels can.

He echoes Rilke's implication: "a god can do it." Ironic is his answer to the ancient visionary stance, which consisted of asking the help of the Angel, as an intermediary between man and god.

The connection of fiction with artifice is expressed more overtly in "Someone puts a pineapple together," which concludes with "Here the total artifice reveals itself / As the total reality."

150

The basic image of "fiction" is most striking because it is less doctrinaire in *The Rock*, where we see bare rock first and then rock unexpectedly draped with leaves. In a neighborhood of houses that the poet is revisiting after seventy years, which betrays many signs of impermanence, there looms a high rock covered with leaves, and the poet conjectures the blooming of the potentially colorful flowers; we do not know whether the leaves on the bare rock are part of the conjecture to whose meaning he leads us:

> The fiction of the leaves is the icon
> Of the poem, the figuration of blessedness
> And the icon is the man.

The meaning is clear if we use the process of substitutions in the symbolist *écriture*: the fiction is the power of creation, the icon is the symbol, the writing is a divine act, and the poem is what survives of the man. The whole philosophy of the fiction of the poet is there in terse terms. The stark elements of nature that become the instruments of the poet's imagination create his fiction. There is not even the dichotomy between the intellect and imagination, or the struggle between the self and the soul that we observed in Yeats and Valéry because like Mallarmé, Stevens has as an agnostic shed such dualities, and he has even gone beyond Mallarmé's haunting awareness of an absence. With no god to lead him, art is the guiding light of his existence.

> The essential poem at the centre of things, . . .
> But it is, dear sirs,
> A difficult apperception, this gorging good,
> Fetched by such slick-eyed nymphs, this essential gold
> ("A Primitive Like an Orb")

For Stevens art is not the vision of a consciousness ascending but rather of descending toward the unconscious, as in Mallarmé's *Igitur*. The purpose of art is to find a substitute for

151

nature even when employing the elements of the physical universe, just as the bird of Byzantium turned "golden" or Mallarmé's reed turned musical. Like his predecessors Stevens combats a void of which he is certain. His detachment from that void, as its scribe, recalls the hermetically evoked cabinet of Mallarmé in his sonnet in rhymes of "-yx." The absent space is the violet abyss of Stevens under the surveillance of an Angel, reminiscent of Rilke's and not of Swedenborg's. The semi-god of Mallarmé's *Afternoon of a Faun* had power beyond reality or even beyond the dream; and Rilke, in envisaging the powers of the created poem, had suggested that godlike powers had been reinvested in the poet.

Stevens needs only the Angel in his frequent references to the necessary angel or ephebe. In "An Ordinary Evening in New Haven" and in "Angel Surrounded by Paysans" the figure is elaborated. He is an inhabitant of "man-locked" earth, "a thing by the side of a house, not deep cloud":

> The ephebe is solitary in his walk
> He skips the journalism of subjects, seeks out
> The prerequisite of sanctity, enjoys
>
> A strong mind in a weak neighborhood and
> A serious man without the serious
> Inactive in his singular respect
> ("An Ordinary Evening in New Haven")

How close this is to the meaning of poetry, according to Mallarmé, in avoiding "the journalism of subjects"—yet the sacerdotal function loses its French elitism in "He is neither priest nor proctor" and "enjoys the strong mind in a weak neighborhood." This is a secular angel no longer suspended in an in-between world as in Rilke's poetry.

Here the poet is in direct, if jocular, competition with the notion of angelic action. Later, in another poem, called "Angel Surrounded by Paysans," a still more intimate attitude is taken toward the Angel. It can be noticed that Stevens used the word

152

"paysans" when he could just as well and more normally have used the English equivalent. Could it be that he was suggesting the new connotation Rimbaud had given the word "paysan" when he identified himself as a paysan in *Une Saison en enfer*, where he was referring to a primarily pristine creature unburdened of conventional sight and sound?

As Stevens elaborates his description we find an American democratization of the angel as we did of the priest/poet—a factor not perceptible in any of the European counterparts of this poetic self-portrait.

> I have neither ashen wing nor wear of ore
> And live without a tepid aureole
>
> Or stars that follow me . . .
> I am the necessary angel of earth
> Since, in my sight, you see the earth again

Real and earthy is the angel presented by Stevens as if in retaliation for all previous angels; yet in the second part of the poem, the ephemeral character is wrapped in a liquid element and the apparition assumes an oracular ambiguity of speech—"like meanings said / By repetition of half-meanings"—and there is a forewarning of rapid disappearance: "quickly, too quickly I am gone."

If Mallarmé indulged in the misappropriation of ancient myths, if Rilke gave us a more human Orpheus, and if Valéry's Narcissus was less vain and more inquisitive, Stevens demystified fictitious personae much more radically in his search for new fables. The function of the Angel was not to endow the poet with visionary powers of another existence but, quite to the contrary, to make the visible a little harder to see. We are far from Mr. Tate's interpretation of the mystique of Symbolism as a form of medieval symbolism but much closer to the spirit of Mallarmé and those poets who, coming a generation later than the school of Symbolists, may have understood his meaning and expression on a more intricate and deeper level.

153

In general, beyond the quiet agnosticism that connects Stevens with Mallarmé, there is a search for an immanence in the concrete world of things to overcome the beastly nature. There is also a linguistic affiliation—or shall we call it a common perversity—shared by the two that makes for evident similarity of process even where there are not always encounters of meaning. Stevens, like Mallarmé, enjoys misusing words, tricking the reader by lexical substitutions. But, kinder than Mallarmé, after disturbing the reader he often gives clear definitions of the new significations he has created for derouted signifiers.

Stevens is a self-conscious poet, a theoretician like the French poet. But like Yeats, and perhaps even more so, he is inclined to direct philosophical statement within the poem itself, whereas Mallarmé separates statement of theory from the poem that embodies it. On the contrary, we must admit that in the case of Stevens his theories very often go far beyond what is materialized in the poem itself.

But let us not forget that a determining factor in perceiving "influence" in its constructive sense comes through what is collectively rejected as well as what is assimilated. Stevens, along with the others in this poetic cluster of postsymbolists, rejects the last vestige of anthropocentrism in the cosmos—*without making it a philosophical angst or a political rebellion.* His philosophical stance is coupled with a linguistic one as he sheds the heavy baggage of connotations attached to the common signifiers of poetic discourse—principally, as we have seen, to words and automatic implications such as of Nature, angel, reality, and that most attacked of all literary techniques by the symbolists, description:

> Description is revelation. It is not
> The thing described, nor false facsimile
> It is an artificial thing that exists
> In its own seeming, plainly visible
>
> ("Description without Place")

154

Above all, what brings these poets together is the desperate need to survive in their work after they have lost all other hope of personal immortality. The theme of the survival of the work over the artist is explicit in its analogy of the relation between the planter and the fruit:

> The wild orange trees continued to bloom and to bear
> Long after the planter's death

The tree survives the planter, the icon, and the man. Taking up the same leitmotif in *The Rock*, which carries the themes of Mallarmé's *Tombeaux*, Stevens leaves on the rock, as we have seen, the poem, which is both the icon (the work) and the man. Reminiscent of Valéry's *Le Cimetière marin*, it represents, however, the cyclic regeneration of the work instead of the renewal of the life element in nature as suggested by the cemetery poem of the French poet. The reflowering of the plants on the rock is more directly in keeping with the notion proposed by Mallarmé that the work renews itself as time moves on. Rock becomes identified with the resilience of art in relation to the vulnerability of the artist himself. The quality of the work makes it immortal as it is projected into objective views distancing itself from the corporeal, tangible being by whom it is engendered.

In "Of Mere Being" Stevens evokes an ever-singing bird at the edge of space very evocative of Yeats's golden bird of Byzantium and of the general perpetuity of the poem. In this sense he adhered until late in his life to the theory launched by Mallarmé that the symbol in poetic structure has the power to survive what it signifies.

However, as one reads the poetry of Stevens not in fragmented quotable dictums but in its flow and continuity, it becomes difficult to distinguish between the artifice of the poet and the encircling power of Nature. The poet chose Connecticut over New York, unlike Mallarmé, who chose to relocate from the provinces to Paris permanently. Natural reality pressed its suit persistently on Stevens. The poet became an Ear and an Eye for Nature, and the creative process became a collaboration. Perhaps war also brought home the unavoidable reality of "civilized" living. He could not sustain for his entire life—which turned out to be considerably longer than Mallarmé's—the vision of disappearing without sails into the unanswering cosmos. His metaphysics became less remote, as he explained in *L'Esthetique du mal*:

> And out of what one sees and hears and out
> Of what one feels, who could have thought to make
> So many selves, so many sensuous worlds,
> As is the air, the mid-day air, was swarming
> With the metaphysical changes that occur,
> Merely in living as and where we live.

The final affirmations of Stevens are in tune with those of Valéry's "Il faut tenter de vivre" and with the hope poems of Jorge Guillén, and of other conciliatory poets who accepted the cosmos if not the human condition.

What Stevens preserved of the cult of Symbolism was the discrete demeanor of the poet in society; but whereas Mallarmé thought of society as hostile to the purposes of poetry, Stevens adjusted better to the social as well as the physical reality. He cultivated imagery as a channel for the transformation of reality but never quite reached the core of language, never quite revealed its intricacies or sought to take full advantage of them. In the course of time he got closer to his fellowmen, and thereby it was harder for him to fictionalize the universe. If he solicited the assistance of homely angels and ephebes, they were not the glowing forces of the "génie" evoked by Rimbaud, nor did they have the vulnerable evanescence of Rilke's Orpheus. If Stevens utilized colors as presences in an invisible world they do not carry the catalytic forces of the orange of Rilke or the azure of Mallarmé. If like Valéry he looked in mirrors he saw himself as he was and not as a creature of the interspace. He did not develop the terror of the abyss as did his French colleagues. The symbolist fiction affected his language more than his being. His poetic fiction and his daily reality eventually converged into an indivisible unity.

Jorge Guillén

HIS BATTLE WITH THE CRYSTAL

THERE ARE exterior elements that bind artists together—such as a prevalent mentality, social attitude, and politico-historical events. There are also internal strata formations resulting from the parallel intellectual developments in individual artists of separate national cultures. Certainly such was the case with poets who all made Baudelaire a twentieth-century poet and identified with him without necessarily identifying with one another. The third and most binding tropism is that of direct impact, constructive influence that catalyzes and then transforms what is acquired in relation to what is innate or ingrained unconsciously.

The Spanish poet Jorge Guillén, who outlived the rest of this cluster of poets and spanned several generations and modes of poetry, qualifies on all three counts in this cohesion and thereby invites inclusion in this group, whose kinship transcends national literary and spiritual barriers. Guillén shares with Valéry, Rilke, Yeats, and Stevens the familiar paradigms and the linguistic developments that disrupted traditional practice of poetic representation and analogy.

The cloud of agnosticism passed over Guillén as it did over a whole era of artists, regardless of their particular form of expression, who were brought up in the concept of the fin de siècle and came of age in a catastrophic world. It was a time when most writers had to make a basic choice between engagement in social reformation, translating that militancy into artistic ruptures and transformations, and a withdrawal into the art form as a world apart.

159

Modernists, such as the Dada group and the surrealists, cubists, and expressionists, went the way of confrontation. Others—principally those examined here as postsymbolists—receded into the universal self that overcomes the vicissitudes of the moment by finding an inner leverage. Valéry declared that the ivory tower had never been higher. For Yeats there was an inner rift of personality that produced an upsurge of political expression, but more often his craft tended to absorb the circumstances into a universal analogy. So aware was Guillén of belonging to a group larger than the conventional classification of "generations" that he describes the coalition of the larger group as "we poets," transcending divisions of age or ethnic formation when he says in his own introduction to the bilingual selection of his *Cántico*, "We were all of us speaking in images." And the totality of his work evidences the wider-than-national parameters of his relationships by including references and tributes to all the poets in this seriation, and others that one could associate with them.

In the second category of cohesions, these poets read Heidegger or his popularizers, absorbed a philosophy of immanence, and were supported by the notion of the potential plenitude of the experience of temporary reality. This was a distinct departure from the essentialist perception of the Cartesian "je pense donc je suis" interface of metaphysical poetry, manifest in classical and Romantic traditions.

Rilke's German as well as Guillén's Spanish had ways of grammatically asserting the distinction—the former with the manipulation of "Sein"/"Dasein," the latter with "ser"/"estar." As pointed out in reference to Stevens, poets using English and French had to interpolate the difference more indirectly. Hence both in Valéry's work and in Paul Claudel's—from totally different points of view—the struggle to express distinction can be identified through the Latin *Animus/Anima*.

But even more important than their common philosophical orientation was the fact that they all read Mallarmé and his derivatives in the Symbolist Movement. What separates them, however, from the practitioners of the conventional symbolist *écriture* is their return to the source in terms of both theoretical position and poetic practice, demonstrated by their use of the substitution strategy, already noted in the other poets, and their misnaming and fictionalization of physical reality. This was, as I have been illustrating, a process they discovered in Mallarmé's major poems better than in the Master's immediate successors who elaborated on the letter rather than the spirit of synaesthesia, instrumentation with words, and symbolization.

On the third level of contact, the mitigating factor that creates variations in the personal encoding of *écriture* has to do with the diversely stacked literary portfolio with which each was endowed. Valéry, the heir apparent of Mallarmé and the one most directly connected with him, was nonetheless removed by a generation of poets whose manipulations of verse diverted them from the Mallarmé contact and the fruition of his own major writings. His indecision as to the direction he would take is apparent in the fact that twoscore years of silence were to pass between Valéry's theoretical writings and their major expression in poetry.

For Rilke the pull of the German Romantics inevitably diluted the purity of the Mallarmé source; as for Yeats and Stevens, the English heritage coexisted and created a contrapuntal escape from the symbolist structure.

Jorge Guillén's universality has been only belatedly recognized, and he has yet to achieve what he so dearly desired—to have his works collected into a single unit, the ultimate Book,[1] a standard edition. The first three volumes appeared as a single book in an Italian edition as *Aire nuestro*, but his *Otros poemas* and *Final* were never absorbed with the earlier works as he had hoped. For, like Mallarmé, he firmly believed in the integrity of the Book. Moreover, he has not yet had a major critical study of his work to put the parts of the mosaic together. The various shorter studies on Guillén that have appeared agree that he is to

---

[1] See Mallarmé, "Quant au livre," 369.

be classified with the Spanish generation of 1927, with which he himself identified; then the filiation is taken back to the Spanish mystics of the seventeenth century, to San Juan de la Cruz; and the fact that Guillén did an edition of Fray Luis de Léon's *El Cantor de la Cantare* that corresponded to the vulgate *Canticum Cánticorum*[2] gives everybody ample proof of his major inspiration. Furthermore, he is associated in form with Luis de Gongora. If we are able to accept these findings we cannot follow this thinking to the point which Gustavo Correa, the author of one important study, makes: that in view of these Spanish influences Guillén is diametrically opposed to Mallarmé and the Symbolists, whose work "contains an obsessive negativism and nihilism."[3] More analysis of that "negativism" as it relates to Mallarmé and more probing into the nature of the "affirmation" of Guillén may present a picture different from the current assumptions.

Guillén's most enthusiastic admirers are diffident when any hint of other affiliations is discerned in his writings. His closeness to Valéry, who was more than twenty years his senior, is well known and indisputable. Guillén not only wrote about the French poet but translated him, and was particularly noted for his rendition of *Le Cimetière marin*. It is, therefore, curious that his commentators should unanimously want to diminish this factor as if it took something away from his personal value. Ivar Ivask expresses the consensus when he says, "one can . . . miss Guillén's originality by perpetuating the legend of the poet as the student of Mallarmé and the translator of Paul Valéry, the propounder of *poésie pure*."[4] But it is not a "legend." The contact is a fact[5] and it does not deter from Guillén's originality but rather enriches his work by enhancing its dimensions. It is the

[2] See Gustavo Correa, "La Poetica de la Realidad," in *Homenaje a Jorge Guillén* (Madrid, 1978), 123.

[3] Ibid., 125.

[4] See Ivar Ivask, "The Impulse toward Form," in *Luminous Reality* (Norman, Okla., 1969).

[5] Professor Claudio Guillén, the poet's son, makes a cogent statement on

confluence of filiation and affiliation that gives his work its spe-cial mark—and, in spite of similarities with his own Spanish generation and his acknowledged place in Spanish literary his-tory, it relates him to the postsymbolist group with his own special rendition of the features that have emerged in the com-parative study of their collective work.

There are objective reasons for the right to disengage Guillén from his generation, although he remained loyal to the end to his Spanish heritage. Generally, Spanish poets tend to be insular, with the kind of pride in distancing themselves and cultivating their uniqueness that is also evident in the British. But there is, in contrast, an ubiquity in Guillén that took him to France, Italy, and the United States, as well as to many other countries. The geographic data had cultural repercussions. The *Cántico*, his major body of poems, from whose nucleus addi-tional poems from various stages of his life grew, was begun in Brittany, and there is a savor of France in the intonation of the Spanish idiom. He had a remarkable mastery of several foreign languages (which he ceased to treat as "foreign"), and he dedi-cated many of his poems to a roster of foreign poets both living and dead. All these elements draw him into the common pool of those who, in theory and practice, fictionalized material real-ity into their poetry.

The linguistic strategies in Guillén's poetry follow closely the pattern of Mallarmé noticeable in the other poets—princi-pally, the tactic of substitution of denotations in a consistently sustained interchange. We shall look at some of these examples. Another device is in the nature of syntactical idiosyncrasies that permit priority arrangement in linear form of concepts and im-ages to be highlighted. In Spanish, Guillén is able to do in a much more acceptable way what Mallarmé did in French. One

---

this issue. He says: "On Valéry you are quite right. What happened is that some literary historians kept hammering on this affiliation in a tiresome way and so my father liked to stress in conversation that Valéry was very much a formalist and not inclined to any thematic affirmation of life."

of the elements of Mallarmé's style that makes the reading so difficult and the meaning so hermetic is his Latinized sentence structure in which reversals of the order of infinitives, the distance of past participles used as adjectives from the substantives they qualify, and the displacements of prepositions and adverbs give him the priority system he has chosen for his words but make his sentences very unnatural and almost in need of parsing. Valéry had observed how, to the horror of his readers, Mallarmé extricated his poetic language from the standard rules of syntax that demand a self-effacing compliance on the part of language to communication—that is, to cede priority to the thought it conveys.[6] Mallarmé had tried, sometimes awkwardly, to free language from this task by superposing his own structures as stumbling blocks that make the reader stop and take notice of the language as a goal rather than as a tool.

For the Spanish poet who wants a similar personal arrangement for his priorities of meaning the process is more normal because the Spanish structure is more permissive, more pliable, and allows more choice for the shuffling of word order, thereby allowing a hierarchy of reader attention to the relative importance the poet assigns to the communicated meanings in the poem. Often, unfortunately, the subtle process is destroyed by translators who do their own reshuffling. If observed closely, Guillén's poetry reveals a process similar to Mallarmé's but less ostensible because of the more supple form of the normal Spanish sentence structure.

In Guillén's poetry the use of adjectives with the power of nouns is also reminiscent of Mallarmé. "Más fuerte, más claro, más puro / Seré quien fui" echoes "le vierge, le vivace et le bel aujourd'hui." It is the alternation between "el" and "lo" that gives so much flexibility to the substantive quality of the adjective: "el intruso," "el sediento," "lo esperado," "lo vivido," "lo más real," and so on. In a language in which one can easily be-

---

[6] See Valéry's article on Mallarmé in *Paul Valéry: An Anthology*, trans. Malcolm Cowley and James R. Lawler (Princeton, n.d., 170) Bollingen edition.

come loquacious, Guillén preserves the terseness of Mallarmé and Valéry.

In examining these linguistic resources, we come now to his lexicon. The most pervasive word usage is his handling of "ser" and "estar" to convey his philosophy of immanence, essential being, and human plenitude of experience. We have already noted the parallel device in Rilke's handling of "Sein"/"Dasein" and the difficulties in language that cannot avail themselves of this convenience.

To convey similar distinctions Valéry had to resort to a secular use of the *Animus/Anima* designation. In his treatise on *L'Ame et la danse* the separation was suggested by the insertion of the image of "flame" as the intermediary between essential intellect and the repository of experience, the tug-of-war between possibility and event, which Guillén achieves through the direct power of transition between the signifiers "ser" and "estar." In his seemingly simple little poem "Ser," the struggle between *Animus* and *Anima* occurs in purely poetic form. It illustrates what Valéry called, in the words of Eryximaque to Socrates, "L'âme s'apparaît à elle-même, comme une forme vide et mesurable" [The soul appears before itself like an empty and measurable form] ("L'Ame et la danse," 2.168). The participation of "l'âme" for Valéry in the work of the artist, represented here as the dancer, causes "extrême félicité," rendered, in similar circumstance, by Guillén with less redundancy in the single word raised to the highest power—"felicísimo." Valéry groped and tried to define "l'âme" in a secular manner (the equivalent of "ser") in paraphrases:

L'âme est bien ce qui n'existe pas: ce qui fut et qui n'est plus—ce qui sera et qui n'est pas encore;—ce qui est possible, ce qui est impossible—voilà bien l'affaire de l'âme mais non jamais, *jamais*, ce qui est! Et le corps qui est ce qui est.

[The soul is indeed what does not exist; what was, and what is no longer—what will be and is not yet, what is possible, what is not possible—that's the problem of the soul but *never*, *never* what is! And the body which is what is.] (2.171)

165

Valéry has to introduce an agent in the interaction of the soul with the physical performer, an intermediary object designated as "flame" or "étincelante salamandre"—which he characterized as the action of the moment that is between the earth and the sky. This is one of his many efforts in his total work to substantiate the in-between world of poetic fiction.

Guillén needs only the interplay of the subtlety that his language offers him—from "ser" to "estar," for example, in the poem "Ser":

> El intruso partió. Puedo ser donde estoy
> Ya nada me separa de mí, nada se arroja
> Desde mi intimidad contra mi propio ser.
> En él quien se recobra dentro de un cuerpo suyo
> Felicísimo como si fuese doble el alma.
> Juvenil, matinal, dispuesta a concretarse
> El contorno dispone su forma, su favor,
> Y no espera, me busca, se inclina a mi avidez,
> Sonríe a mi salud de nuevo ilusionada.
> El intruso dolor—soy ya quien soy—partió.

> [The intruder left. I can be where my experience takes me
> Now nothing separates me from myself, nothing usurps
>   henceforth
> My intimacy from my own being
> The one that recovers from its own body
> The peak of felicity as if the soul were double
> Youthful, matinal, ready to become concrete
> Its contour determines its form, its pleasure
> And it does not wait, it seeks me out, it copes with my greed
> Smiles upon my reillusioned self-fulfillment
> The intruding grief—I am what I am—has left me.]

The intruder that mysteriously opens the poem is identified in the last line as "dolor." The culprit is life itself, which emerges as an intruding impediment to the work of the creative artist. "Ser," or *Anima*, takes on the vulnerable being. The

166

bondage is sealed in the confluence of the inner self with the outer self, giving concrete form to all the shape (poem) that the artist covets, in his self-illusioned sense of fulfillment that enfolds in the identity of the intruder, which is grief—a reality of life—self-revealed in the last line. And because in Spanish "intruso" can be an adjective as well as a noun, it now finds itself the qualifier of grief. But as the intruder departs there is a suggestion that the artist is triumphant when he identifies himself with his artist self. This interaction between the physical self and the creative self is illustrative of an element that recurs frequently in Guillén's poetry.

But neither the translation nor the paraphrase can convey the interplay, the sense of intimacy the poet expresses without revealing the personal nature of his grief. No explanation can fully convey the process of conquering the grief that is going on throughout the poem nor, above all, the process of creation inherent in the line "El contorno dispone su forma, su favor"— that is, the movement from sketch ("contorno") to completion ("forma"). It is an apt instance of the theory dear to Valéry that philosophy can be incrusted in the language, which then becomes realization rather than merely representation—what Valéry expressed in prose as "an idea of some *self* miraculously superior to Myself."[7] Guillén embodies this concept as the coming together of "soy" and "estoy."

There are many instances in the work of capsule philosophic lines where the thought is lodged succinctly in the language— "El caos fué, no será," in "Mundo en Claro," or "el alma en la piel," in "Anillo"—or of an ontology of immanence that communicates prismatically as words do in Mallarmé's *Un Coup de dés jamais n'abolira le hasard*: "Absoluto de instantes," in "El Concierto" and in so many others.

Among substitutions, notable is the use of the word "crystal." It stands for glass, windowpane, the window itself, mirror, and simply for an unclassified luster-generating element. "Tras-

---

[7] *Anthology in Poetry and Abstract Thought*, trans. Denise Folliot, 115.

parancia" is often associated with crystal. Crystal also sometimes has the meaning of "rosace" without the religious connotation. And it relates to "sky," which is often a foil that comes into play with crystal, and the latter is substituted for "azul" as "azur" is for Mallarmé. In his long poem "El Aire," air is identifiable with purity as Guillén associates crystal with transparence both physical and spiritual:[8]

Un frescor de trasparencia
Se desliza con un tempano
De luz que fuese cristal
Adelgazándose en cérifo

[The cool transparent air
Glides like an ice floe
Of light—was it crystal once?
Then tapers to a gentle breeze]
(translated by Hugh Creekmore)

A close look at a key poem, "Una Ventana," will bring out some of the features perceived in relation to Mallarmé's "Les Fenêtres" and "Azur":

El cielo sueña nubes para el mundo real
Con elemento amante de la luz y el espacio
Se desparaman hoy dunas de un arrecife
Arenales con ondas marinas que son nieves.
Tantos cruces de azar, por ornato caprichos,
Están ahí de bulto con una irresistible
Realidad sonriente. Yo resido en las márgenes
De una profundidad de transparencia en bloque.
El aire está cinendo, mostrando, realzando
Las hojas en la rama, las ramas en el tronco
Los muros, los aleros, las esquinas, los postes:
Serenidad en evidencia de la tarde.
Que exige una vision tranquila de ventana.

[8] In *Cántico: A Selection—Spanish Poems with English Translations*, ed. Norman Thomas di Giovanni (Boston, 1954).

Se acoge el pormenor a todo su contorno
Guijarros, esa valla, más lejos un alambre
Cada minuto acierta con su propia aureola,
¿O es la figuracion que sueña este cristal?
Soy como mi ventana. Me maravilla el aire.
Hermosura tan límpida ya de tan entendida,
Entre el sol y la mente! Hay palabras muy tersas,
Y yo quiero saber como el aire de Junio.
La inquietud de algun álamo forma brisa visible,
En circulo de paz se me cierra la tarde,
Y un cielo bien alzado se ajusta a mi horizonte.

[The sky dreams up clouds for the real world
With the warm element of light and space
Dispersed are now the dunes and reefs
Drifting sand making sea waves like snow mounds
Sometimes random crosses, to adorn artifacts
Forming shapes yonder with an irresistible reality.
I dwell on the margins of a pit of transparence—a block
The air is closing in, displaying, making the leaves glimmer
In their branches, and branches in their trunks
The walls, the eaves, the corners, the poles,
Manifested serenity of an afternoon
Which calls for a window vision of tranquility
Detail is induced in all its contours
Pebbles, that fence, further on a barbed wire
Or is it a configuration dreamed by the crystal
I am like my window. The air enhances me
Such limpid beauty already in an accord
Between the sun and the mind
These are very terse words
And I want to be wise like the June air
The stir of some poplar, visible breeze formation,
In a circle of peace the afternoon closes on me
And a sky nicely vaulted accommodates to my horizon.]

For Guillén, as for his predecessor, "window" is a prismatic object carrying multiple analogical undulations; for Mallarmé

169

it is the art symbol that opens out on escape into something larger even than art—"Que la vitre soit l'art, soit la mysticité" [May the glass be Art, be mysticity]—and at the same time it is a barrier from which the reality of Man, represented in "Les Fenêtres" as an ailing figure, recoils: "Mais hélas! Ici-bas est maître" [But alas, the here and now is the Master]. And he envisages himself as a frustrated human, a bird without wings: "Est-il moyen / D'enfoncer le cristal . . . / Et de m'enfuir avec mes deux ailes sans plume?" [Is there a way to break through the crystal? And to fly away with my two featherless wings?]. Art is not a sufficient means of transcendence in "Les Fenêtres," and yet in "L'Azur," although the rebellion may be useless, he is haunted by the azure: "L'Azur triomphe." In these two poems that represent his waverings, rather, Mallarmé suggests his incertitude in two conflicting movements—one away from reality into the embrace of art, the other toward an ambiguous but luminous chaos. Guillén's direction is surer, a straight line between the sun and the mind of the poet.

It should be noted that these are early poems of Mallarmé, and the symbolism and techniques are direct, overt, in spite of several innuendos and suspended developments of thought. Ironically, the window poem of Guillén is closer to the mature style and technique of Mallarmé than to Mallarmé's own azure poems. For Guillén the window vision is in concordance with nature's creativity, and yet instead of being a barrier to transcendence, it is a representation of the poet's creative process as well. Nature and poetic artifice do not produce tension, but intermingle. If the sky dreams up clouds, the atmosphere contributes to the artifact, as the sun to the image-making mind of the poet. The famous turning point of Rilke's vision here becomes the marginal space occupied by the artist who has to conciliate depth (which is opaque) with transparence: "Yo resido en las márgines / De una profundidad de trasparencia en bloque." Untranslatable is the contact of the four signifiers margin/profundity/transparency/block. Margin suggests minimal space, profundity gives a vision of abysmal and limitless space, transparence annihilates the opaqueness of profundity only to be caught by the concrete and even more opaque presence of block.

But as Guillén further demonstrates in "Mundo en Claro," the crystal is triumphant over darkness as he again brings together the images of crystal and window:

> Lo oscuro pierde espesor
> Triumfa el cristal. La ventana
> Va ensanchando hasta el confín
> Posible la madrugada,
> Flotante en una indolencia
> Que no es mía. Todo vaga.

[Darkness becomes weightless / The crystal triumphs. The window / Stretches all the possible / Confines of the dawn. / Which floats in an indolence / That is not mine. Everything wanders.]

This long poem is Guillén's *La Jeune Parque*. Guillén, like Valéry and a whole generation of unversed but fascinated initiates to the functioning of dreams, which had become popularized by Freudian psychology, thinks of dreams as the last frontier of human experience. He tries to express in language that is concrete the semiconscious passage into darkness and the return from the oblivion of the unconscious to awakening. In both poems diffidence and struggle are suggested on the way to the unconscious state and an analogy is established between the return of the sun and light and the return to consciousness. In the case of Guillén the analogy of the in-between state with the struggle of the sun to break out of darkness into dawn is the central image of the poem and precipitates the sense of glorious triumph of the poet. It is interesting to note that in neither poem is the falling into the dream state a cult of the mysterious in itself; rather it is a testing of the poet's ability to *return* and to assume *control* over his vision. Whereas the early Symbolists tried to make the clear object mysterious and endow the dream image with intention, Guillén communicates the ineffable in solid imagery but leaves immense gaps of connections. As a result the vision remains private in spite of a seemingly direct communication. So the effect of dream creates its own world in which there occurs a constant shuffling of the forms and their ordinary relationships. Had Guillén spaced these signifiers in the nonlinear form of a page, he would have produced a kinship not with Mallarmé's early poems but with *Un Coup de dés*.

The struggle between light and darkness is coded into words such as "alba," "alborozo," "alborear," and a number of other expressions of dawn, such as "madrugada," from other roots. The concept of things as both objective and subjective realities brings into emphasis the simple word "cosa," constantly, but with it "forma," and, as we have seen, "contorno"—all leading to the principle of what truth is: "verdad" and "verdadero," and a semantic transcendentalism that is achieved with the constant use of "más" and "allá" and adjectives raised to the superlative power, and, as we have already noted, the juxtaposition of "ser"/"estar" to encapsulate a philosophy of immanence and transition.

In the *Cántico*, even when the poem is not primarily about the transition between sleeping and waking, the poet is in an interworld between dream and the wakeful state. His "entersueños" in "Mundo en Claro" parallels Rilke's "Zwischenraum." Guillén's vigorous sense of impermanence gives the present moment a composite content: "Todo es ahora"—Man in transit, constantly transforming his "ser" into "estar"; "Estar es renacer" in "Paso a la Aurora," or "O jubilo / De ser en la cadena de los seres, / De estar aquí" in "Más Verdad." Verge and passage are privileged moments that are expressed not in direct philosophical statements but in movements between objects (reality) and dreams or created objects expressed as "forma"— "Entre las cosas y los sueños / Avanzas" in "Más Vida"—detachment from personal being deemed necessary to view the cosmos. And at times he conveys the sense of being alone in the cosmos just as Mallarmé did in his sonnet through "-yx," but more often he suggests through the use of the second person the presence of a companion as he tackles the physical reality of an indifferent "cielo" or "firmamento" (too often conveyed by his translators into the English "heaven," even though there is no evidence in his verse that he is seeking recourse to divinity).

Guillén mediates the notions of time and space, shaking, as it were, the disorder of the universe to compose his own rules. A whole philosophy relating to the battle between nature and the artist is entrenched in the compact line "El muro cano / Va a imponerme su ley, no su accidente," in "Muerte a los Lejos." The physical reality of death, so grippingly conveyed in Rilke's Vera poems as an open gate, is here the white wall. "Muerte a lejos," as the title implies, is the distance the poet is placing between his vibrant, living self and the ultimate end, which will eventually cause him to disappear. But the important privilege the poet claims even at the final moment is that his demise not be an object of "chance." Like Mallarmé he struggles with "azar." He bargains for the universal law, here named "accidente," but wants to avoid the chance element as long as possible.

MUERTE A LOS LEJOS

> Je soutenais l'éclat de la mort toute pure
> —Valéry

Alguna vez me angustia una certeza,
Y ante mi se estremece mi futuro.
Acechándole está de pronto un muro
Del arrabal final en que tropieza

La luz del campo. ¿Más habrá tristeza
Si la desnuda el sol? No, no hay apuro
Todovia. Lo urgente es el maduro
Fruto. La mano ya le descorteza.

. . . Y un dia entre los días el más triste
Será. Tenderse deberá la mano
Sin afán. Y acatando el inminente

Poder diré sin lágrimas: embiste,
Justa fatalidad. El muro cano
Va a imponerme su ley, no su accidente.

DEATH FROM A DISTANCE

When that dead certainty appalls my thought,
My future trembles on the road ahead.
There where the light of country fields is caught
In the blind, final precinct of the dead
A wall takes aim.

But what is sad, stripped bare
By the sun's gaze? It does not matter now—
Not yet. What matters is the ripened pear
That even now my hand strips from the bough.

The time will come: my hand will reach, some day,
Without desire. That saddest day of all.
I shall not weep, but with a proper awe
For the great force impending, I shall say,
Lay on, just destiny. Let the white wall
Impose on me its uncapricious law*

(translated by Richard Wilbur, from *Cántico: A Selection*)

In the meanwhile Guillén has created a world that lies in the non–tick-tock instant to which he gives, through the use of language, an uncanny permanence. He achieves this effect by using qualifiers signifying the infinite coupled with time signifiers that are finite: "eterno presente," "Oh presente sin fín," and "Oh absoluto Presente," all in "Anillo," his tribute to love, which does not give intimation of eternity but deals with the finite as if it were an absolute. Designation of objects passes from vague outline into solid form. Guillén accepts but disdains the non-anthropocentric universe upon which he gazes.

* literally, "impose on me its law and not its random chance"

In his mediator role between Man and chaos, he meets, as did Rilke and Stevens, the necessary angel, who is neither a theological nor a mythical one but rather a personal Orpheus figure: "Nada se puede contra el ángel / El ángel es" he asserts in "Más Vida."

As Mallarmé and in his wake the postsymbolists fashioned and used their individual keyboards of words and their substitutes, these became the ultimate cluster of undulated meanings; they took on the function of symbols that surpassed the metaphor and even the metonymy in order to become word prisms. There is such a cluster of words in Guillén, as in the other poets examined in this study. Finally in Guillén there occurs a reversal of the code as he moves from *Cántico* to *Clamor*. This is not simply a chronological reversal but the other face of the coin. To conclude that the affirmation associated with light in *Cántico* becomes darkness and rejection in *Clamor* is too simple an interpretation because affirmation and reality are not unilateral significances in Guillén's work; rather, they are part of a palimpsestic structure.

Commentators who say that Guillén was a realist have passed too rapidly over the fact that reality has a specialized meaning for him. It is not a given but a confection, something he chisels out of raw materials, his own fiction that makes his poetry self-referential, for it represents *his* moments strung together. They create their own continuity in defiance of the fact that at some point they will come into fatal collision with a set of laws outside the jurisdiction of the poet and succumb. The world is a myth for Guillén—his own. There is no objective continuity outside of his control until the fatal end, no narration that would be a compliance with chronological time and its limits, but a series of juxtapositions of *his* moments as they pass from his "ser" to his "estar," or luminous experience. In these presentations (not representations) he is dealing not with variations but with contradictions. The innocent reader will quickly be convinced that he is referring to reality as we gener-

175

ally perceive it, only to find out with repeated delving into it that his reality is the concrete manifestation of the subjective, and thereby is not representative but transformational.

The commitment to this theory is made explicit in the very first poem of *Cántico*. In "Más allá" (which should never be translated as "Beyond," since that word has acquired supernal implications) Guillén means "further on" or "yonder," because "allá" is for him distance in time as well as in space, implying concrete geographic as well as temporal meaning. In this poem he is distinguishing between data-based static reality and the selection of things through which he verifies his being. He depends on things (reality)—"dependo de las cosas"—but without him they simply *are* (passively), whereas through him they take on the significance which turns reality into the virtual images that in Mallarmé's theory are the poet's *fictions*: "Sin mí son y ya están." Taking this concept from objects to humans, they too *become* through his power of transfiguration and thus belong to him more intimately than they ever could as autonomous selves.

Some traditional symbolists absorbed the outer world in a totally solipsistic posture. Neither Mallarmé nor Guillén remains at that level of introspection. Instead both poets return what they have retrieved, creating that *flower* (a substitution for the work of art) absent from all bouquets in Mallarmé's words. The broader meaning of Mallarmé's concept becomes the nonrestrictive image of the identity of flower/poem/artifact disengaged by the poet/artist from limiting context but recognizable in terms of what Guillén likes to call "contorno." Consequently, while it is the one "absent" from the givens, it never becomes *absence, which would be an abstraction with a capacity for annihilation*. The process for both poets is inherent in what Guillén means when he says, "Vaguedad / Resolviéndose en forma." To those, therefore, who would deny the affiliation of Guillén with Mallarmé on the basis of Mallarmé's alleged nihilism against Guillén's affirmative stance in *Cántico*, it can be retorted that the nihilism of the person of Mallarmé should not be confused with the poetic voice that had the power to create *fictions* that defend a higher reality *here* and *now*—which is the most profound meaning of art itself.

In fine, belief in a new ontology of artistic experience non-representative of accepted norms of reality, produced by the combination of the data of the senses (through the eye and the hand) and filtered through the dream, is the greater truth Guillén perceives in his poem "Más Verdad"; its actualization is subject to the *Word*: "Esa verdad que espera a mí palabra," that is, "mis torsoros de imagénes" [my treasure of images]. In a mutual transfusion, he invents reality after reality has invented him so that he may become its Book: "La realidad me inventa / Soy su leyenda" [Reality invents me / I am its reading material]. The naming that becomes the substance of that reading creates "Maravillas concretas" and is protected from philosophical abstractions. All the objects Guillén names in his idea of "más verdada" are concrete though undefined entities: "El balcon, los cristales, unos libros, la mesa" [The balcony, the crystal, the books, the table].

In "El Aire," another long poem of affirmation, a signifier such as the abstract and often-used "trasparencia" is associated again with "cristal," which is fused first with air/zephyr and then with mirror, and in another poem, "Cara a Cara," it is linked with ivory, and finally alights on a window: "El defensa es el cristal / De una ventana que adoro." As we have already noted, the enemy of vision, of life, of creativity is named "accidente," the element of disorder that the poet combats all through *Cántico* in relation to both his craft and his very life. The drama of the conflict comes to a head in "Cara a Cara."

In a sense Guillén is as skeptical as Mallarmé in believing that the creative order—that is, the "coup de dés"—will not banish the ever-threatening "chance" (azar/suerte/accidente) but will hold it afar as long as possible. He will with stubbornness repeat "Aqui estoy," "Yo no cedo / Nada cederé al demonio," in "Cara a Cara," and then again—"No soy nadie, no soy nada / Pero soy—con unos hombros / Que resisten y sostienen /

Mientras se agrandan los ojos / Admirando cómo el mundo / Se tiende fresco al asombro"—with which the poem ends.

Because of that resistance, when he considered death more realistically, he opposed "aquí" [here] to "Muerte a los lejos" [far]. And when it comes it will be according to laws and not accidentally, even if those laws are beyond his jurisdiction as an artist.

As noted in reference to Valéry and Stevens, the conciliation with the world occurred at a certain point in their life course and in their work. This change has generally been observed to have taken place in Guillén's poetry as he moved from *Cántico* to his later *Clamor*. It has been said that his earlier work was an affirmation of life, whereas the later ones fall into a darker mood brought about by the onset of the Spanish Civil War and the coming of World War II. These world-shaking events, however, do not enter directly into his poetry—which, like the rest of the works of the poets here explored, remains on the whole uncircumstantial, notwithstanding the fact that all these poets had made statements in prose about what Valéry called "La crise de l'esprit" [The crisis of the mind].

But in all these cases, "darker" is not a sign of rebellion but rather one of conciliation with reality as understood by the world at large. *Clamor* is a dark intonation but an acceptance of ordinary reality in its uncrystallized sense, so that if the mood is dark the poet's situation is closer to that of his readers and, therefore, ironically he achieves more direct communication with them. This appraisal can be verified structurally by juxtaposing some of his later poetry with the earlier work.

In examining the computerized word-count study of Elsa Dehennin,[9] which relates principally to Guillén's later work, it is surprising that the author herself is not concerned with the word "crystal." Her rundown of prominent words, however, shows clearly the virtual disappearance of that signifier from

---

[9] Elsa Dehennin, "Des Mots-cles aux configurations stylistiques," in *Homenaje a Jorge Guillén* (Madrid, 1978), 185–211.

the later work. But what is more interesting, when it *does* appear it is *devaluated*. The comparison of the following two poems makes the distinction dramatic.

The poem "Presagio" is not only a "symbol" through its title but is symbolic of Guillén's philosophy in *Cántico* and contains all the elements that have been signaled in what preceded:

Eres ya la fragancia de tu sino.
Tu vida no vivida, pura, late
Dentro de mi, tictac de ningún tiempo

¡Que importa que el ajeno sol no alumbre
Jamás estas figuras, si, creadas,
¡Sonadas no, por nuestros dos orgullos!

No importa. Son así más verdaderas
Que semblante de luces verosímiles
En escorzos de azar y compromiso.

Toda tu convertida en tu presagio,
¡Oh, pero sin misterio! Te sostiene
La unidada invasora y absoluta.

¿Que fué de aquella enorme, tan informe,
Pululacion en negro de lo hondo,
Bajo las soledades estrelladas?

Las estrellas insignes, las estrellas
No miran nuestra noche sin arcanas
Muy tranquilo se está lo tan oscuro.

¡La oscura eternidad oh! no es un monstruo
Celeste. Nuestras almas invisibles
Conquistan su presencia entre las cosas.

OMEN

This moment you are the fragrance of your fate
Your life as yet unlived, pure, beats
Within me a tick tock of inexistent time

What matters if the alien sun will never
Illuminate these figures, doubtless created,
But not dreamt, by both our prides!

No matter. Thus they are truer
Than the faces of improbable lights
In perspectives of commitment and chance.

All of you converted into omen,
Oh, but without any mystery! You are sustained
By the invasion of unity, absolute.

What became of that enormous, so amorphous
Swarming in the blackness of the deep,
Under the star-filled solitudes?

Those illustrious stars, all those stars
Do not look toward our secretless nights
There is much quiet for so much obscurity.

The darkness of eternity, oh! is no celestial
Monster. Our invisible souls
Conquer their presence among things.

(translated by Claudio Guillén)

In this poem Guillén is confronting the indifferent, non-an-thropocentric universe supported by an alter ego, surely a loved woman,[10] unlike the solitary stance of Mallarmé. He super-poses on the unknown character of the cosmos his *created* im-ages and their clarity for him. Instead of being overcome by the mystery around him he proudly ("orgullo") asserts his own challenge. He also rejects all but subjective time, that inner time that is measured for him within the scope of the living presence of the beloved: "Tu vida no vivida, pura, late / Dentro

[10] I had originally put "probably a loved women." Claudio Guillén sug-gested that I change it to "surely," and made the following observation that will be of interest to the reader: "He was very conscious of woman, of the erotic poem, as a touchstone, as a crucial manifestation of the constructive relation with reality."

mi, tictac de ningún tiempo." He defies that light of the sun that does not reach those images he has created and that are not even objects of dreams, so stark and concrete is their reality. They are also truer than the truths of chance. The defiance is expressed in two exclamations of "Qué importa" and "No importa," and the juxtaposition of "Verdaderas" with "verosimiles" is exactly the opposite of what we expect because what Man creates is generally considered to be "seemingly" true ("verosimile") whereas what is in the universe is presumably the pure truth. Here, instead, the creation of the poet contains more truth than what is outside. Finally there is a return of that dread word we saw already in "Presagio": "compromiso," associated with "azar," the chance that Guillén said elsewhere will overcome us but that is to be avoided as long as possible.

In the next verse all the dichotomy of the "here" and the "yonder" is reversed: unity and the absolute are of our making, loneliness is the plight of the stars and not ours, the incomprehension ("arcanos") is in the stars and not in us, and we can contemplate the obscure universe that is neither monstrous nor celestial, for our seemingly invisible souls grasp (as if to ask whether anyone doubts their existence because they are not visible like the stars) the presence of eternity through the presence of things.

The simple "entre las cosas" is linguistically ambiguous because one has to wonder if "cosas" is being used self-referentially to mean the "figuras" he created; in that case, we have to infer a totally subjective reality in which "entre" acts like the crystal symbol of an object of prismatic visibility. Or is Guillén projecting the more usual notion of the macrocosm manifest in the microcosm, which would direct the reader to view eternity in, among, and between the cracks of the empirically experienced world? I tend toward the former interpretation because I do not see elsewhere in the poems of Guillén the philosophic notion that the universe is contained in a grain of sand, and because the first explanation I have suggested makes the change we shall encounter in the following poem a more striking one.

To match the defiance of the earlier "Nuestros dos orgullos," we end here on the note of conquest with "Conquistan," which has more force if we believe that the universe of the speaker is superior to the given because it is of his own making and that "cosas" are not random objects but what he called earlier in the poem "estas figuras, sí creadas" (the insistent "sí" emphasizing the fact that they were created exclusively for him and his companion).

Now looking at a short poem, "Vista y Vision," from *Homenaje*, his last collection, in the light of the tragic and mortal elements he conveys in *Clamor*, we have a reversal of language-connotation as well as of philosophical position:

> Este cristal—candor de abril muy frágil—
> Acoge con placer y fiesta al rayo
> Que su júbilo trae de tan lejos
> Cristal propicio a luz que lo atraviese
> Guzan los dos—y yo—de esa amistad
>
> Encantándonos siempre está el enigma
> Que al intelecto acucia sin rendirle
> Su clave. Luz, pudor! Pudor arisco
> Nos vela a toda luz ahí los mundos,
> Inaccesible a vision, a mente.

The crystal here is *de*crystallized in terms of its earlier meaning: it has become a candid figment of April (which refers back to the earlier but more enthusiastic use of April) and it is fragile as spring, subject only to light that comes from afar and is, it seems, intended for their sense of amicable togetherness—for again the poet is not alone. Having limited the power of crystal, he now comes to the important difference in the last stanza, which can be rendered approximately as follows:

> Still enchanting us in this enigma
> Which beckons to our intellect without delivering
> Its key. Light, timidity! Faintness of this timidity
> Which veils all light of yonder world
> Inaccessible to our vision or mind.

182

The reader will note that "orgullo" has been replaced by "pudor" (which may be translated also as "reticence"), the enigma and its inaccessibility has been acknowledged, the power of the crystal has not only waned but thereby brought about a division between vista (objective) and vision (subjective), giving the former a dominance over the latter and its controller, the mind or interior being. It is a poem of concession and not of conquest.

This may be a "darker" poem but it is also suggestive of a more realistic world in the same sense as the final stanza of Valéry's *Le Cimetière marin*: "Le vent se lève. Il faut tenter de vivre." We accept life and its consequence. It marks a curb from his fictitious world to the *consented* one of everyman, and it could be said that ironically his proclamation of affirmation of life was an affirmation of life as seen by the artist, whereas the so-called darker affirmation is a more conforming one, following the same direction as noted in the older Wallace Stevens, who accepted life and its limits in his Connecticut environment. A world that still promises vistas but restricts visions could be considered a greater affirmation of reality because it brings the artist into the fold of a more universally accepted one. It all depends on the angle from which one views that ambiguous word *reality*.

As has been noted with regard to the other poets in this cluster, the postsymbolist cohesion is also only a *partial* feature of the totality of Guillén's work. His conciliation with the world, as in the case of Stevens, is one of the differences that emerge. What also and more distinctly sets Guillén apart from the symbolist mood is the element of an *open* eroticism, a more personal drawing toward an exterior object of that love, an alter ego in the female companion. Not named specifically, she is the silent responder to many of his queries that the reader does not hear but presumes. That silent but acquiescing voice is what decreases for the poet the terror of the white door.

Guillén's life adventure was more complete than that of any of the others here associated with him. The introversions noted in Mallarmé, Rilke, and inherent in Valéry's obsession with

Narcissus are not part of his personality and, therefore, are not reflected in the structure of his poetic writings. His poem "A lo Narciso," for instance, is one of appreciation but also one of distancing.

In the development of his poetry, Guillén gradually abandoned even his terseness, and in that sense the more open style parallels the increasing amplitude of his long life experience and brings him closer to Saint-John Perse, Jules Supervielle, and, as some believe, even Walt Whitman.

It is interesting to note that although Guillén was a very visual poet in his imagery, he used music and sound as the analogue of his two most important titles. The obsessive need of all these poets to create a nonrepresentative art form in literature in emulation of music—which heretofore has been the only art that had achieved that feat—was the basic motivation of the call to the musical lexicon: "La Poésie, proche l'idée, est Musique par excellence," said Mallarmé in *Variations sur un sujet*. So it is *Cántico*, the structured musical creation, where Guillén collects poems in which he has fashioned a parallel and not a reality representative of the one lived; but it is *Clamor*, or unstructured noise, that is representative of the *accidental* character of the universe when he has conceded to its supremacy.

If Mallarmé is seminal then Guillén is a corrector of the human condition, a conciliator who makes if not his peace then at least an armistice with reality. He savors that splendor of the moment as something beyond the purely aesthetic pleasure communicated by the symbolists. Without the naiveté generally associated with earthy poets, Guillén expresses spirituality within the context of the sensual. Appropriating the "gozo" of physical involvement in life, he knows but does not unduly deplore its ephemeral quality.

Love and music are in his poetry overt proclamations that take him beyond the mysteries and ambiguities of relationships and the intricacies of composition. If at times he is engrossed in the sophistication of creative process, which brings him into kinship with Mallarmé, he is open to the glories of *effect*, in terms of the harmony of love and of music. He is no Prometheus aiming for the power of gods, and therefore, consciousness of his mortality, ever present, is not accompanied by obsessive frustration.

Reasonable, normal, serene—these are attributes not often associated with poets, particularly those who have ventured into the darkness of the cosmos and the self and returned somber like Baudelaire, ascetic like Mallarmé, fragile like Rilke, or cabbalistic like Yeats. Instead, Guillén comes out of the Orphic journey fortified by equanimity.

Surely, his "Anillo" is one of the great poems on love in modern poetry, and "El Concierto" is the summation in a voice ringing loud and clear of all the cumulated fascination and seduction that a century of poets had experienced in their efforts to master the secrets of music, which they deemed the most perfect of the arts because it is the most independent of the dictates of any exterior reality.

Guillén also tells us that the intricacies of thought need not necessarily be cast in intricacies of language. In pursuit of that "fiction" in poetry that has meant a disdain of truth as the populace understands it, he has not felt that as a consequence he had to veil the communication of his "más verdad" from his readers. The solitude that becomes an exigency of the search for the poetry of language has not overflowed in his case into his personal relationship with the world and has not dimmed his sense of communication. He constantly created bridges between his formulation and its avenues of dispensation.

There is no waiting in terror for the day of doom. And because the apprehension of that "Muerte a los Lejos" does not reach a state of panic, his lyrical power identifies in a single voice without having to project his attitudes and images on phantoms or legendary figures such as Igitur or Hérodiade.

There is no trace of schizophrenia. Guillén would be a disappointing case study for psychocritics because there is a superb balance and a confluence of exterior objects and phenomena, subject to mortality, and an interior wisdom to stabilize the unpredictable ("accidente") with what his powerhouse of intellectual vigor can sustain of his *forms* so that things are the richer for it: "Canto / De formas que sí consiguen / La perfeccion del momento" ("El Aire").

It is ironic that this most cosmopolitan of the six figures here included was to have received the narrowest reader response as of the end of the twentieth century, particularly outside his own country. Surely the immense output of this major poet, whose dissidence is ontological rather than political and whose magnificence is so accessible, will break through the barriers of translation to give answers and be a "hombro" in their meditations on the crucial problems of life, which as their major contribution the Symbolists and postsymbolists deemed to be the only legitimate function of the poet. Placed at least *partially* in the postsymbolist context, both his affiliation and his originality may become more manifest.

Conclusion

THIS CLUSTER of some of the major poets of the Western world stands in jarring isolation when viewed in the light of the reaction that has become prevalent at the end of the twentieth century to the effete, evanescent, elegiac attitudes of the white male figure of poetic lyricism of what appears to many readers to be an archaic past.

In short, the ultimate question that haunts anyone undertaking microcosmic inquiry is whether it can make any impact on our perception of the macrocosm of literature. How does the measurement of intensely experienced moments in time relate to the chronological passage of time in an era—even a century—in reshaping the features of a civilization one hopes is still cast in clay and not yet constricted in stone, since in clay it can still change?

Does the eschatological data gleaned from these readings lend greater credence to the poetics involved? If history is a response to event, then literature is a response to the effect of event on our perception of human destiny.

When I read in the current commentary that the computer has created an "artificial reality" I have to murmur, "Had not the poet done so years ago?"

But let us look beyond the literary in the writings of a group devoted to the literary. Out of the six figures involved, from the self-referential view of their texts, four lived long enough to turn from introspection to recognition of the world around them and to the need to reach out to their contemporaries.

Valéry's *Regards sur le monde actuel* was his pessimistic appraisal of what civilization held in store for his generation. If Stevens said, "the death of one god is the death of all," Valéry mused that the death of one civilization was the death of all. Yet, having said at the end of his elegy *Le Cimetière marin*, "Il faut tenter de vivre," Valéry did try to keep looking ("regards") around him and relating to what was left of the society that had taught him better to look *within* himself and that led him to vaster spheres to measure *without*.

Jorge Guillén, who could delineate his interior topography in the far reaches of Brittany, remote from his place of birth, was drawn in later years toward the need to identify with his native land, and also desired to address himself to a larger spectrum of readers. To them he conveyed a stoical optimism suggestive of a human transcendentalism rather than of the possibility for divine ascension.

Yeats went perhaps further than either Valéry or Guillén in terms of the development of a social and political presence. As quoted earlier, he resolved to become an active and ordinary man instead of a visionary, replacing the teleological with a more practical vision of life on this planet.

Stevens chose among the ways to look at a blackbird a routine way of viewing life, suburban and stable, rooted in lifestyle rather than routed for adventure.

Mallarmé and Rilke died too young to have had an opportunity to decide on a change of course, but one can wonder if with some twenty more years of life they would have lifted their heads out of their feathers. The barrier between life and art was greater and stronger, and their very definition of "to live" was an elsewhere undefined, lying somewhere between physical life and the supernal; they were not quite sure what they had rejected or what they had opted for, which makes "change" more difficult than impasse.

But whereas the authors of the texts we have clustered were not necessarily compatible through their personalities and aspirations in the way their writings are associable, the larger meaning of their works throws light on a cohesive mentality that troubles the end of the century rather than bringing insight into their personal problems or attitudes.

Let us recall some of these cohesive factors reflected in their writings rather than in their lives. Rilke's fascination with the Orpheus legend is in its point of emphasis very pertinent to the question of human choice. In the formal myth, Orpheus is given a second chance to recapture what he has lost—that is, his beloved Eurydice—on condition that he not look back. To my knowledge all evocations of that myth in the arts have highlighted the pathos of the impatience of Orpheus, who does look back and then loses not only his beloved but life itself, at the hands of the Furies. In Rilke's *Sonnets* there is no concern expressed about that part of the legend nor with the dismemberment of Orpheus. Looking back is not the answer to our nostalgia for the beauty that is gone, nor is death the ultimate solution to our grieving. What matters is what Orpheus will leave behind permanently—Orpheus *after* the mortal attack, surviving in his work, communicating after returning from the metaphysical journey "from that bourn from which no traveler returns."

Was that not also the perilous descent of Mallarmé in *Igitur*, which he subtitled "the Folly of Elbehnon?" Was that not the secret agenda of the Symbolist ontology—to convey a mystery independent of theological topographies, to sever and preserve the sense of mystery and the sense of the sacred beyond their previous commitments and their dogmatic delimitations?

In Swedenborg's philosophy of transcendence there is an intermediary angel who guides the way. For the poets here discussed, the figure survives as a new version of a ghost image but loses divine attributes. Rilke's and Guillén's angels, Yeats's Druid, Stevens's ephebe are all necessary companions in the plotting out of the trajectory of verbal illumination but are earthbound, on a par with the poet, transposable to the ever-present human need for "the other," whether in Freudian interpretation of the superego, or in the dialogue between self and soul, or man and his art, or the larger substitution of what is retrievable in our performance in life and what vanishes forever, like Eurydice.

189

And this brings us to the many references to stone: Mallarmé's "porphyre," Rilke's lute in stone, Valéry's monuments affixed on top of the shadows of the dead, Stevens's flowering rock, Yeats's marble hall emptied of the dancing human figures. Stone, which since time immemorial was associated with the mark of human death, and which became the archaic emblem of closed civilizations, suddenly took on the signification of life transcending death, and thus assumed the power of communication as a gauge of human resilience.

This kind of signal of transcendence is not a promise but a challenge, the second chance—the art that may survive the artist, as we have seen defined through a series of substitute designations for the extended meaning attributed to "artist." But for the reader who does not practice any form of the arts, and who also partakes of that universal desire for the second chance, there emerges the concern for the human legacy, the extralegal endowment of the human to enhance what has to be passed on, the second chance not to waste the treasure but to hand it down with a bit more luster and a bit less mire.

One realizes that the most significant eschatological character of the writing in question is the problem of Narcissus. The standard myth tells of the penalty of self-admiration: to be transformed into a pretty but futile flower at the edge of a stagnant pond. The Narcissus factor of self-examination immanent in this body of works is not indicative of the reflection of an accurate mirror image. Valéry's Narcissus avoids the penalty as Rilke's Orpheus combats total annihilation. Valéry sees something more than self in the dialogue with Narcissus; the subconscious, as it has sometimes been described in its Freudian impact on Valéry, is a pool of second chances, a self-transcending promise whereby the self and the Other create still another, synthetic being eligible for survival.

Finally, interwoven throughout this reading of what appears to be a fictitious world created by the artist as a substitute for the rejected one of the naturally perceived reality, is the vastest of all the themes it stirs: that of fatality versus the human will to choose. To invent nonspecifiable spaces or indeterminable time perceptions, to divest nature of its decaying process, to give new meaning to old myths, constitute inherently a struggle to fight fate. But the pathos that interferes with an obstinate choice to create one's own sphere of existence is in the premonition that "the young parqua" is indeed a new form of fate of man's own doing that could be more treacherous than the wrath of gods.

These poets have indeed fashioned their own fiction in creating an anachronism that is totally out of touch with "l'esprit nouveau," which was being declared by other voices of their time. They constitute in the post–World War I era a beautiful Byzantium that promises to keep their splendor intact when their voices have been silenced and their values extinguished.

André Malraux said at the end of his *Imaginary Museum* that the work of art through the centuries is marked for sleep or survival. If, ironically, we discover eternal truths in forms considered archaic and by formers who are gone, the fiction of the poet can well become an ongoing reality since the greatest change of venue of twentieth-century perceptions is based on its discovery that reality is a variable, and is open-ended in form and matter. Their fictitious world has become, in ways they never dreamed, a part of reality within the widening and more permissive concept that the imaginary is but one step ahead in the progression of the real.

❖ *Index* ❖

accident, 6
aestheticism, Parnassian, 79, 81
Afternoon of a Faun, The (Mallarmé).
   See *Après-midi d'un faune, L'* (Mallarmé)
"Aire, El" (Guillén), 168, 177, 186
Aire nuestro (Guillén), 161
allegory, 5
"A lo Narciso" (Guillén), 184
ambiguity in meaning, 15, 18; in
   Mallarmé's poetry, 28–29, 37–38,
   39, 51; in Rilke's poetry, 84–85,
   90, 93, 94; in Valéry's poetry, 54,
   55–56, 67, 70; in Yeats's poetry,
   105, 110–12, 117, 121–22
Ame et la danse, L' (Valéry), 165
"Among School Children" (Yeats),
   119
analogy: demise of, 5; in neosym-
   bolist mode, 7
"Anashuya and Vijaya" (Yeats), 111
Ancient Gods, The (Cox), 34
"Angel Surrounded by Paysans"
   (Stevens), 152–53
"Anillo" (Guillén), 167, 174, 185
Apollinaire, Guillaume, 71, 86, 141
Après-midi d'un faune, L' (Mal-
   larmé), 29, 43–49; compared to
   Stevens's poetry, 152; compared
   to Valéry's *Fragments du Narcisse*,
   62, 63–65, 66; compared to
   Yeats's poems, 117, 118–19, 130
Arbre, L' (Valéry), 56, 57–58
architecture, and poetry, 53, 54–58,
   65
Arensberg, Walter Conrad, 136
A Rilke pour Noël (Saint-Hélier), 80
art, and truth, 56
"Assis, Les" (Rimbaud), 26
"Autumn of the Body, The" (Yeats),
   25, 105

avant-texte, 29–30n.4
Axel (Villiers de l'Isle-Adam), 104,
   112
"Azur, L'" (Mallarmé), 168, 170

Balzac, Honoré de, 72
Banville, Théodore de, 44
Barrès, Maurice, 59
Barthes, Roland, 33
Baudelaire, Charles-Pierre, 26, 49,
   66, 82, 95, 129, 135, 137–38,
   159, 185
Beckett, Samuel, 6
Benamou, Michel, 22, 134n.2, 140
Bergson, Henri-Louis, 72
biography, and explanation of po-
   etry, 21–22
Blake, William, 21, 122, 124, 132
Block, Haskell, 114–15n.6, 132n.2
"Blood of the Moon" (Yeats), 121
Bloom, Harold, 103, 141, 142, 144
Boucher, François, 44, 62
Brémond, Henri (l'abbé), 60
Breton, André, 15, 16, 71n.3, 141
"Brise marine" (Mallarmé), 26, 30,
   73
Burt, E. S., 4n.2
Byzantium symbolism, 125–27
"Byzantium" (Yeats), 125, 127–29

Calligrammes (Apollinaire), 71
Cántico (Guillén), 22, 160, 163,
   172, 175–79, 184
Cantor de la Cantare, El (Léon),
   162
"Cara a Cara" (Guillén), 177–78
Cazalis, Henri, 32
"Celtic Element in Literature, The"
   (Yeats), 105
Chassé, Charles, 33
chronos. *See* time

time (*cont.*)
  poetry, 112, 113, 118–19, 126, 128
"Toast funèbre" (Mallarmé), 50
Tombeaux (Mallarmé), 42, 49, 50, 99, 155
"Tower, The" (Yeats), 117–18
tower symbolism, 121
Traité de Narcisse (Gide), 62
transformation. *See* metamorphosis and transformation
tree symbolism, 57, 66, 68–69, 90, 98, 143
Trembling of the Veil, The (Yeats), 109
tropes, neosymbolist mutation of, 6–7
Troy, fall of, 130, 131
truth, and nature, 56
turning point (in time), 33, 119, 170, 178

unconscious, 19–20, 41, 59, 63, 72, 74–75, 151
unicorn symbolism, 95–96, 100

Valéry, Paul: and ambiguity of meaning, 54, 55–56, 67, 70; architecture in poetry of, 53, 54–58, 65; as atemporal, 71; and construction, 54, 76; and cult of the self, 58–60, 62–63, 66, 70; and extensions of symbolic images, 16; and fate of humanity, 71–76, 187–88; and French literary heritage, 21, 66, 69–70, 78; influence of Mallarmé on, 53, 56, 58, 142, 161; influence on American poets, 139; influence on Guillén, 78, 162–63; influence on Rilke, 78, 79n.1, 80; and intention, 65; music, dance, and architecture as nonrepresentational models for, 54–56, 85; lack of interest of, in representation, 53; and Orpheus

myth, 65, 67, 69, 75, 77; as postsymbolist poet, 4, 19; and purity, 68, 75; turning away from symbolist mode, 20; and turning point, 33, 178; use of "artifice" by, 53–54; use of language by, 60, 160, 165–66
—works of: *Ame et la danse, L'*, 165; *Arbre, L'*, 56, 57–58; *Cimetière marin, Le*, 58, 77–78, 99, 155, 162, 183, 188; *Eupalinos*, 55–56, 57; *Fragments du Narcisse*, 61, 62–69, 76; *Introduction 133 la Méthode de Léonardo da Vinci*, 56; *Jeune Parque, La*, 55, 57, 58, 59, 61, 70–77, 171; *Narcisse parle*, 68; *Narcissus*, 59; *Philosophie de la Danse*, 54; *Regards sur le monde actuel*, 187
Variations sur un sujet (Mallarmé), 16, 184
Vendler, Helen, 103, 148n.6
"Ventana, Una" (Guillén), 168–69
Verhaeren, Emile, 134, 135, 137
Verlaine, Paul, 25, 116, 137, 140, 145
"Vierge, le vivace et le bel aujourd'hui, Le" (Mallarmé), 17, 26–27, 29, 37, 49, 86, 97, 123, 164
Villiers de l'Isle-Adam, Auguste de, 104, 112
Villon, François, 37
Viollet-le-Duc, Eugène-Emmanuel, 148
Vision, The (Yeats), 21, 111
"Vista y Vision" (Guillén), 182–83
visual arts as nonrepresentational model: for Mallarmé, 34, 39–40, 47, 48, 54, 55, 85, 86, 89, 145; for Stevens, 145–46, 149, 150
Voltaire (François-Marie Arouet), 32
"Voyage, Le" (Baudelaire), 95